BACK TO THE ETHIC

Reclaiming Western Values

Diane Weber Bederman

Published by:
Mantua Books Ltd.
Canada
www.mantuabooks.com
Email: administration@mantuabooks.com

Library and Archives Canada Cataloguing in Publication
Bederman, Diane Weber, author
      Back to the ethic : reclaiming Western values / Diane Weber
Bederman.
ISBN 978-1-927618-05-9 (paperback)
      1. Christian ethics. 2. Jewish ethics. 3. Ethics in the Bible. 4.
Civilization, Western. 5. Liberalism. 6. Democracy.
I. Title.
BS680.E84B43 201   241   C2015-907839-3

Cover Illustration and Design by Jodie Goldberg.

To my father Abraham and my mother Sarah; to my
children and grandchildren and all who follow; and
always, Marc.

Like apples of gold inlaid with silver is a word that is aptly spoken.

Proverbs 25:11

CONTENTS

ACKNOWLEDGEMENTS

This book would never have been written without the encouragement of my therapist, who said to me: "Just do it!"

Thank you, Rabbi Reuven Tradburks, for lifting me up when I was in the abyss.

A heartfelt thank you to Peter Stockland, editor of *Convivium*, who published my first article—a piece from this book—and who has continued to publish my work.

Thank you to Doug Swenson, who created my website (www.dianebederman.com).

Thank you to Marni Soupcoff for bringing me on board with *Huffington Post Canada*. Thank you to the *Times of Israel* for embracing my blog and to Judi McLeod for giving me the opportunity to contribute to *Canada Free Press*.

Howard Rotberg—you read my book and said yes! And to J. P. Brooks—a writer is only as good as her editor. You have made this book far better with your wordcraft.

Last but not least, a special thank you to Jon Stewart and Bill Maher, whose public disdain for religion encouraged me to complete this book.

INTRODUCTION

*The heart of your culture
is your religion: Christianity.*

*. . . The Christian moral foundation of social
and cultural life was what made possible . . .
the successful transition to [Western
democracy]. We don't have any doubt of this.*

—A Fellow of the
Chinese Academy
of Social Sciences[1]

*[The ethical system we received from the Jews is]
incomparably the most precious possession of mankind,
worth in fact the fruits of all other wisdom and learning put
together*

**On that system and by that faith there has been built
out of the wreck of the Roman Empire the whole of our
existing civilization.**

—Winston Churchill

We are living in an era of dis-ease. Our belief systems are under attack. We witness the horror of terrorism spreading in countries who do not share our values, as well as the spread of terror in democracies around the world. We are up against tribal societies whose ethic is one of honor and shame and where blood revenge is in the veins, where violence begets violence that, over time, can lead to a sense of helplessness, hopelessness, and victimhood. At the same time, too many of us born into freedom have become apathetic to, even neglectful of, the very ethic that underpins that freedom.

---

[1] Ferguson, *Civilization*, 256.

There are approximately seven billion people in the world. Of those 3,046,158,000 people, 43 percent live in flourishing democracies and 23 percent, or 1,613,858,500, live in countries designated as *Partly Free*: "[a country] in which there is limited respect for political rights and civil liberties. *Partly Free* states frequently suffer from an environment of corruption, weak rule of law, ethnic and religious strife, and a political landscape in which a single party enjoys dominance despite a certain degree of pluralism." The other 34 percent of humanity live in countries designated *Not Free*.[2]

The findings of "Freedom in the World 2013," an annual survey done by the organization Freedom House, show that over the course of 2012 more countries lost freedoms than gained them. It is the seventh year in a row in which countries with declines in freedom outnumbered those with gains. "As in the world at large, more countries in the Middle East and North Africa (MENA) region endured declines than made gains in their drive toward freedom in 2012."[3]

Loretta Napoleoni, in her book *The Islamist Phoenix,* suggests that "the promise of a radical Salafist state whose borders trace those of the ancient Caliphate [is] a more powerful motivation than the will to 'spread democracy'."[4]

Thailand reverted to military rule in 2014; Recep Tayyip Erdogan of Turkey took away his country's freedom of the press; Russia under Putin has returned to its old one-party system of authoritarianism; and China continues to attack dissenters.[5]

Democracies are fragile, and difficult to maintain. Winston Churchill, a champion of democracy, wrote: "It has been said that democracy is the worst form of government except all the others that have been tried." I suggest it is either due to arrogance or naiveté that far too many people in democratic countries believe

---

[2] Arch Puddington, "Freedom in the World 2013," Freedom House, https://www.freedomhouse.org/ sites/ default/ files/ FIW%202013%20Booklet.pdf.

[3] Ibid.

[4] Loretta Napoleoni, "The ISIS Seduction," Full Comment, *National Post,* January 5, 2015, http:// news.nationalpost.com/ 2015/01/05/ loretta- napoleoni- the- isis- seduction/.

[5] Jeffrey Simpson, "On Balance, A Tense Year in Geopolitics," *Globe and Mail,* December 20, 2014, http://www.theglobeandmail.com/globe-debate/on-balance-a-tense-year-in-geopolitics/article22152105/.

that the other four billion people on this planet yearn for our way of life. Many don't.

> *This might surprise you, but the*
> *freedoms we have come from the Bible:*
> *the blueprint for democracy.*

This might surprise you, but the freedoms we have in the West come from the Bible: the blueprint for democracy. Biblical ethical monotheism, revolutionary when brought into our collective consciousness 3,500 years ago, changed us from tribal societies incapable of caring for other people into a culture based on free will: a culture that has evolved over time and remains to this day evolutionary. Yet there are well-educated people in our society who attack religion, as if religion were only dogma and creed, as if religion and the sciences and humanities are diametrically opposed. They are not.

For those of us who believe in God, the Bible adds wonder and awe to our way of living. The stories in the Bible are layered with meaning that speaks to our minds and our souls. These powerful Bible stories teach all of us about human behavior. Most important, they teach us the prerequisites for the establishment of democracy: how to become moral and ethical human beings, able to live in a compassionate, moral, and ethical civilization.

Along with social justice and prophetic law, the Bible gave us our Western understanding of the sacredness and sanctity of life, of our uniqueness as well as our commonalities: the freedom and the obligation to make individual choices rather than merely sit back and accept whatever fate is handed us by our society. This book of laws, the Bible, gave us the fundamentals of our court and justice systems and business law. It gave us the command to care for the animal kingdom, because it admonishes us to recognize that all of God's creations are "beautiful and glorious." We are told: "Take care that you do not corrupt or destroy My world."[6] We are reminded over and over that we are a part of this world and we are responsible for what happens in it.

---

[6] *Midrash Rabba*, commentary on Ecclesiastes 7:28.

Sadly, we are losing our connection to the Bible's ethical rules, and are thereby putting our Western democracies on life support. Not only are we under attack from those who hate our way of life, but our Western culture is crumbling from the internal pressures of worshiping the false gods of absolute tolerance, inclusion, and accommodation to the point that we welcome beliefs, customs, and rituals that undermine our democracy—in the name of democracy!

> *Somewhere along the way to political correctness nirvana, God and religion became four-letter words.*

Somewhere along the way to political correctness *nirvana*, God and religion became four-letter words. We stopped teaching the potent biblical ethic to our children years ago. I went to a public school where a passage from the Bible was read to us every day. Not to proselytize, but rather to teach the ethic. We must reclaim and internalize that ethic. We must return to that teaching, to the words of the Bible, words that bear great fruit, because the root of Western democracy *is* ethical monotheism; it is the foundation upon which Western culture sits. As Aristotle teaches us, "Educating the mind without educating the heart is no education at all."

And millions of people have died to defend this culture, this ethic, these freedoms. The religio-ethic of the Bible, the Judeo-Christian ethic, demands of us that we be our brother's keeper and that we care for the other person as we care for our brother. But this cannot mean that in the name of caring for others we let tolerance of their foreign ways—such as the denial of human rights for women, sex-selection abortion, or honor killings—overwhelm us to the point that we lose our own culture. As Thomas Mann observed, *when it is evil that is tolerated, then tolerance is a crime.* And there is evil in the world. We cannot afford to believe, or worse, to act, as if this is not true.

But we are becoming complacent, taking our freedom of movement and mind for granted because we intrinsically know, when we awake every morning, that we can gather in public places and speak our minds, spreading our words through a plethora of media platforms. We don't think twice about our right to choose those who will lead us, because we know that we can change those leaders through free elections. We have the right to practice our religion in peace. We can choose where we wish to live, when we want to move, and with whom we wish to share our life.

We take for granted the freedom to say, "No." Think about that: we have the amazing freedom, as well as the right and the responsibility, to say "no." No, I won't work there. No, I won't do that; it goes against my moral convictions. No, I won't dress that way. No, you will not send me to another country to be a bride to a stranger. No, I won't stay in this marriage. No, I will not leave school at ten and go to work. No, I won't sit in the back of the bus. We have the freedom to choose.

The former Archbishop of Canterbury, Lord Carey of Clifton, recently lamented: "For too long we have been self-conscious and even ashamed about British identity. By embracing multiculturalism and the idea that every culture and belief is of equal value, we have betrayed our own traditions of welcoming strangers to our shore. Multiculturalism . . . has led to [honor] killings . . . and Sharia law."[7] We must not confuse cultural pluralism with cultural relativism; we must not confuse being warmly open and accepting with being foolishly naive.

Within the leaves of my book you will find compelling reasons to reclaim our founding ethic, to make it your own, protect and defend it, so that you can pass it down to future generations. Through personal anecdotes interwoven with history, psycho-social sciences, philosophy, theology, and science, I want to help you reconnect intellectually and spiritually with the ethical teachings of the Bible, the root of Western civilization.

The stories in the Bible speak to the stresses in our complicated and dispirited modern lives. They remind us of our ethical and moral beginnings and the need to embrace them in every generation. The Bible contains the greatest story ever to unfold: the

---

[7] Matthew Holehouse, "Multiculturalism has brought us honour killings and Sharia law, says Archbishop," *London Telegraph*, August 24, 2014, http:// www.telegraph.co.uk/ news/ worldnews/ middleeast/ syria/ 11053646/ Multiculturalism- has- brought- us- honour- killings- and- Sharia- law- says- Archbishop.html.

story of how the religion and culture of a tribe of insignificant desert nomads changed the way all humanity thinks and feels.[8]

Philosopher Alasdair MacIntyre has written of the importance of stories to the moral life. "Man," he writes, "is in his actions and practice as well as in his fictions, essentially a story-telling animal." It is through narratives that we begin to learn who we are and how we are called on to behave. "Deprive children of stories and you leave them unscripted, anxious stutterers in their actions as in their words."[9]

So come with me as I take you on a journey—back to our roots and then forward in time through stories that will reconnect you to our history. I want you to come away from reading my book with a new appreciation of the Bible as a profound book: a book that makes you question yourself—your moral and ethical values as well as your priorities—that disturbs your equanimity, provokes anxiety, and encourages you to take your place as a caregiver in maintaining our democracy as a free and just society.

First we teach the mind, then we touch the soul.

[8] See Thomas Cahill, The Gifts of the Jews.
[9] Alasdair MacIntyre, After Virtue, 1981, quoted by Rabbi Jonathan Sacks in "A Nation of Storytellers," Israelseen.com, February 4, 2015, http:// israelseen.com/ 2014/09/11/ jonathan-sacks-a-nation-of-storytellers/#more-25288.

I
WORDS THAT BEAR FRUIT

God must be served with the mind, which is
His greatest gift to mankind.

—Bahya Ben Joseph Ibn Pakuda[10]

A democracy can only flourish when there is a tacit agreement by its people on the common rules, values, morals, and ethics that they all must follow. To be a participating member of a Western democracy (and truly to be an upstanding citizen) one must first learn and then internalize ethical monotheism, the Judeo-Christian ethic taught in the Bible. This is because ethical monotheism *is* the underpinning of our Western culture; because the fundamental values of Western democracy come from the Bible.

The Bible itself also teaches us that we humans must internalize our fundamental beliefs. In the book of Ezekiel (2:9–10), God held out an unrolled scroll with the writings of "lamentations, dirges, and cries of grief." And God demanded that Ezekiel eat the scroll, eat the words. Ezekiel was to chew on these words, to internalize them so that they became a part of him, so that he could deliver God's message to His people.[11] So Ezekiel ate the words, and thus incorporated the sorrow and the suffering of God for His people that came from His love for His people. What he ate tasted as "sweet as honey," because he had the opportunity *to taste and see the holiness of God* and to glimpse God's love for His people, even when His people cause Him to suffer. It is not that "lamentations, dirges, and cries of grief" are sweet. It is that love can come from suffering, and love and suffering are all part of the human condition. And just as God comes closer to us in His love and

---

[10] Jacob B. Agus, *The Evolution of Jewish Thought*, 171.

[11] This is similar to the practice in many aboriginal cultures, where eating an animal is a sacred practice. By eating the animal or parts of the animal, it is believed that its traits, such as courage or swiftness, are ingested by the one who has eaten of the flesh; these traits are then thought to become part of the person.

suffering for us, we come closer to God when we experience love and suffering. It is suffering that opens the door to prayer and reflection. So we ask God to forgive us, pardon us, and grant us atonement, and with atonement comes redemption and the opportunity to experience true empathy.

In Roman Catholicism, during communion the participant is believed to be eating the flesh and blood of Jesus, the Son of God. As Jesus said when He blessed the bread and gave it to His disciples: "Take it and eat, this is my body. And then He handed them His cup after the blessing and said, "Drink from this, all of you, for this is my blood, the blood of the covenant" (Matthew26:26–28). This is a physical incorporating of the Son, the most immanent manifestation of God, in order to identify with and internalize the teachings of the Father, to imitate the Teacher and walk in His path, to spread His teachings, His laws, His love. Communion is a constant reminder of the morals, values, and priorities of Jesus. The words of God bear fruit through morality which develops from our constant, conscious choice.

In Judaism, young children are introduced to learning by dipping letters of the alphabet, made from bread, into honey. 'They taste and see the holiness of God,"[12] and associate learning with sweetness, something desirable. They learn the sweetness of the Word of God. "Piety is as the seed that is planted . . . but the final fruit is the emergence in one's heart of the desire to serve God, for His name's sake, not because of hope of reward or punishment . . . for as man's knowledge deepens, so does his piety."[13]

> [Wisdom says,] I love those who love me:
> Whoever searches eagerly for me finds me.
> With me are riches and honor
> Lasting wealth and saving justice.
> The fruit I give is better than gold, even the finest,
> The return I make is better than pure silver.
> I walk in the way of uprightness
> In the path of justice,

---

[12] Agus, Jewish Thought, 264.
[13] Ibid., 173.

to endow my friends with wealth
and to fill their treasuries.

Proverbs 8:17–21

Yahweh created me, the first fruits of His fashioning,
before the oldest of His works.
From everlasting, I was firmly set,
from the beginning, before the earth came into being.

Proverbs 8:22–3

II
TEACHING THE MIND
...TOUCHING THE SOUL

Man raises himself toward God by the questions he asks Him.

—Elie Wiesel

The first thing I do when I see a book is read the blurb on the author. Who is this person? What are her credentials? What do others have to say about her body of work? And the most important question, "Why should I read this book?"

This book began as a response to a personal encounter that appeared to me to be anti-Christian. This encounter, that took place in a small, rural, Christian community, was so egregious that I, a Jewish woman and a multifaith hospital-trained chaplain, was deeply disturbed. How could people living in a Christian community be anti-Christian? (I will share that story in later chapters.) With time to think about it, though, I realized there was much more to the incident.

The real cause was ignorance of the connection between ethical monotheism (the Judeo-Christian ethic), and Western civilization. Due to the different generations, socio-economic levels, and degrees of education in our society, too many people have no knowledge of the influence of the teachings of the Bible on our political and judicial systems. They don't realize that the Bible's instruction to 'care for the stranger' was a radical change in societal relationships: one that made it possible to move from tribal societies to nation-states, to our caring modern societies with publicly funded institutions that are open to everyone.

Immigration brings people from many cultures together in one country. Information travels across our world in real time. In a desire to be accommodating, tolerant, and inclusive, many Western countries welcome these immigrants with their different religious beliefs, traditions, and rituals. But this politically correct ideology of inclusiveness, tolerance, and accommodation is beginning to eat its own young. Those of us who believe in ethical monotheism, one God, and the Judeo-Christian ethic are now treated with disdain and disrespect. We are told that our beliefs are old-fashioned and dogmatic, and so no longer welcome in society.

Many people say that we no longer need to believe in God. After all, the Ten Commandments are just common sense; why would anyone think that murder was right? They say we didn't need Moses to come down from the mountain and tell us something so self-evident. Except that 3500 years ago, murder wasn't thought of the way we think of it today. Moses was speaking in a time when child sacrifice was the norm; revenge killing was expected and accepted; honor killings—the murder of women—were considered appropriate because nothing was more important than protecting the family's honor, and if that meant sacrificing their women, so be it.

To understand that type of society, look at the behavior of tribal societies, today, unable or unwilling to care for "the other," as they open the door to ethnic cleansing and genocide. "Islamism led to the marginalization of non-Muslims." Jews once living in Cairo, Damascus, and Baghdad "have all but disappeared from the predominantly Muslim parts of the Middle East;" Christians, once comprising twenty percent of the Middle East's population, have dwindled to five percent. And the numbers are dropping, as these peoples are forced out by Muslim persecution and war. The diversity among the Muslims in the Middle East is declining, too, as one group cannot get along with the other. Shiites and Sunnis, Wahhabis and Alawites cannot find common ground.[14]

Before ethical monotheism and the revelation at Mount Sinai, there was little concept of the intrinsic value of a human being. There was little concept of the sacredness of human life. It took thousands of years for these novel ideas to become part of the

---

[14] Christian Sahner, "The Arab World's Vanishing Christians," *Globe and Mail*, December 23, 2014, http://www.theglobeandmail.com/globe-debate/the-arab-worlds-vanishing-christians/article22176005/.

DNA of Western culture. That some people think being against murder is just common sense doesn't seem to be preventing us from killing each other, today. I think too many of us take the "self-evident" Ten Commandments for granted.

As I mentioned in my introduction, the majority of people in the world do not live in a truly free society. Our hubris, our ludicrous arrogance, in thinking that almost sixty percent of the world—the two-thirds not living in a democracy—comprehends and appreciates, much less wants, our democratic way of life is deluding us into a state of complacency. How ironic it would be if, years from now, historians wrote that the openness and tolerance of Western democracy was the Achilles heel of Western civilization.

I fear that by the time we wake up and realize that we have completely forgotten the origins of our freedoms, the origins of our right to choose based on our own free will (a paradigm unheard of before ethical monotheism), it could be too late. There is a story of a rabbi needing a miracle, so he found a special spot in the woods, lit a special candle, and recited a prayer. The next morning, his miracle appeared. Years later, a student of this rabbi needed a miracle. He remembered the special spot in the woods, but he did not have the special candle and he was only vaguely familiar with the prayer. So he prayed the best he could. And the miracle took place. Years later, a disciple of that student needed a miracle. He had no idea how to find the special place in the woods, he had no candle, and he didn't remember the prayer. He did not receive his miracle. Why not? Because the story that had been passed down to him through the generations was incomplete. Important information had been taken for granted and was thus lost.

We must learn from this story. It is imperative that we reconnect to our cultural foundation of ethical monotheism, to the Judeo-Christian ethic, in order to safeguard the life and freedoms we take for granted. We cannot afford to forget. In 2011, Niall Ferguson wrote in *Civilization: The West and the Rest*, "Maybe the ultimate threat to the West comes . . . from our own lack of understanding of, and faith in, our own cultural heritage."[15]

---

[15] Ferguson, *Civilization*, 255.

German Chancellor Angela Merkel said, in 2010, "We feel bound to the Christian image of humanity—that is what defines us. Those who do not accept this are in the wrong place here."[16]

In 2013, Charles, the Prince of Wales, cautioned that Christian communities that trace their history back to the time of Jesus are under threat. "We all lose something immensely and irreplaceably precious when such a rich tradition dating back 2,000 years begins to disappear."[17]

> *The ultimate threat to the West comes .. .from our own lack of understanding of, and faith in, our own cultural heritage.*
>
> —Niall Ferguson

And in 2014, Conrad Black wrote, "Our secular leaders in the West, torn between adherence to the agnosticism (or atheism) of most of our media and a mere desire not to offend the fashion, have conspicuously failed to assert Christianity's rightful claim to seniority in chronology, and in intellectual rigor, to all other religions except the closely related monotheistic and messianic one of Judaism. . . . The West is the world's premier center of religious thought and practice."[18] The belief in the Judeo-Christian ethic as the foundation of our country's culture does not mean that others are not welcome to their beliefs and traditions. One doesn't need to be Jewish or Christian to live in this ethical system. The poet Heinrich Heine wrote, "Moses created a nation that was to defy the centuries—a great eternal, holy people, the people of God, which could serve as the model for all humanity."[19]

The Judeo-Christian ethic commands us to welcome the stranger. Yet we are in danger of losing this lifestyle to apathy,

[16] Alan Hall, "Multiculturalism in Germany has 'utterly failed', claims Chancellor Angela Merkel," London Daily Mail, October 18, 2010, http:// www.dailymail.co.uk/ news/ article-1321277/ Angela-Merkel-Multiculturalism-Germany-utterly-failed.html.

[17] John Bingham, "Christianity beginning 'to disappear' in its birthplace, warns Prince of Wales," London Telegraph, December 17, 2013, http://www.telegraph.co.uk/news/uknews/prince-charles/10524211/Christianity-beginning-to-disappear-in-its-birthplace-warns-Prince-of-Wales.html.

[18] Conrad Black, "Defend Christendom," National Review, January 9, 2014, http:// www.nationalreview.com/ article/ 367783/ defend-christendom-conrad-black.

[19] Robert S. Wistrich, From Ambivalence to Betrayal: The Left, the Jews, and Israel, 73.

ignorance, and an unprecedented sense of entitlement that ignores the teachings of social justice and prophetic law: "Do not do to others what is hateful to you."

Some scholars could spend the next millennium philosophizing about our purpose, reason, will, and freedom, and analyzing, justifying, deconstructing, and idealizing these concepts. Many of us, though, find our purpose and our intellectual and spiritual connection to the world through the stories and wisdom of the Bible. Unlike many people, who live with "an open-ended future and the lack of a binding past" and are in "a condition like that of the first men in the state of nature—spiritually unclad, unconnected, isolated, with no inherited or unconditional connection with anything or anyone,"[20] those of us who believe in God and His ethical teachings have come to see and know that we are a part of a larger truth that has stood the test of time.

German philosopher Martin Heidegger (1889–1976) wrote, "Questions are the piety, the prayer of human thought."[21]

I hope that by reconnecting to ethical monotheism and the Judeo-Christian ethic, you will recognize their vital importance to the continuation of Western civilization. Just as Jacob saw himself in a new way, transformed by his wrestling with the angel (see Genesis 32:24–30), I hope that your wrestling with the words of my book enables you to come to cherish the culture bequeathed to you so many thousands of years ago. I hope that my words fulfill your desire to find meaning in your own life, so you can see yourself and your place on the world in new ways. And I hope that you will honor your obligation to be a caregiver of these teachings for those who come after you. First let the words teach your mind, and then they will touch your soul.

As Winston Churchill wrote in 1938,

> It is within the soil of Civilization that freedom, comfort and culture grow. When Civilization reigns in any country, a wider and less harassed life is afforded to the masses of the people. The traditions of the past

[20] Alan Bloom, *The Closing of the American Mind*, 87.
[21] George Steiner, *Nostalgia for the Absolute*, 59.

are cherished and the inheritance bequeathed to us by former wise or valiant men becomes a rich estate to be enjoyed and used by all.[22]

---

[22] Ferguson, *Civilization*, 98.

III
IN THE BEGINNING WAS THE WORD

I feel no attachment whatsoever to organized religion. I see God, rather, as a Creator, as the greatest artist. I see human beings as His most developed artworks.

—Norman Mailer[23]

I know that for those who do not believe in God, it is hard to imagine God speaking and creating. Yet, as a woman of science, I have no trouble living with the uncertainty of the big bang theory of the creation of the universe—or perhaps the multiverse. The big bang theory is beautiful to me: awesome and wondrous in its vision. None of us know what happened just before . . . but we live with that unknowable.

And as a woman of religion, I can also live with the idea of an unknowable God who spoke and brought forward into this world a powerful ethic: an ethic that changed our way of acting in our world in the same way that the big bang theory changed our way of understanding our world. Religion and science need not be antithetical. They each bring reverence and curiosity into our lives—if only we let them.

Human beings have been storytellers across all cultures, from the beginning of time. Through stories, we pass down our knowledge, values, and beliefs. Great stories, great literature, transform us. They make the invisible visible by turning one-dimensional words into multi-dimensional tapestries, tapping into fragmented threads of memory, entering our hidden places, broadening our understanding. Words are like the notes of a symphony, building one upon the other, layer upon layer, speaking to the heart, stirring the blood, reverberating through the chest. That feeling, barely

---

[23] Norman Mailer and Michael Lennon, *On God: An Uncommon Conversation* (New York: Random House, 2007), back cover of book.

contained, reaches a crescendo that erupts: up, out, and around us, to teach our minds and touch our souls.

Perhaps that's what happened to God. He was listening to the music of His ministering angels: the sounds of the trumpets blaring, the tambourines clashing, the clamor of symbols, the sweet sound of the strings, and the soulful sound of the pipes. Then the archangel, Gabriel, blew his horn up into the infinite but empty space. And God was so filled with the emotion of the sounds of the symphony that He could no longer contain Himself and there came from Him this sound, like a Big Bang, and with it, the Word of creation.

Think of great artists such as Picasso and Chagall, whose art changed and evolved over time. The number of canvases they painted, then destroyed, only to be painted again. Or Michelangelo, and the years he spent perfecting his creations on the Sistine Chapel ceiling. Think of Shakespeare with his infinitely creative spirit, his extraordinary perceptions of human nature and behavior, his exquisite use of the English language. Beethoven, whose desire to create exceptional music from a collection of eight notes never stopped, even after he became deaf. There are ballerinas who refuse to stop dancing even when their feet are bleeding. "The miracle of art lies not in the externalization but the conception of the idea."[24] These artists create and recreate as their vision evolves. It is as if they cannot or will not stop their work until they can see that it is good, even very good. It is as if they are compelled to continue until they reach their idea of perfection. Each and every one of these artists is God's partner in the work of creation. Each created something from nothing.

"The beauty of every created thing is the perfection of the work of the master craftsman."[25] Just as all creative artists feel so compelled to create and then recreate, imagine God's compulsion to create an extraordinary world, from nothing into something.

Cosmological theory suggests that the universe began as a primeval point of energy. Through forces as yet unknown, an

---

[24] Will Durant, *The Story of Philosophy*, 515.
[25] Agus, *Jewish Thought*, 288.

enormous release of energy caused space to expand into all we see today. In 1927, a Belgian priest and physicist, Georges Lemaître, first proposed this controversial theory, now known as the "Big Bang" theory. In 1929, astronomer Edwin Hubble noticed that the galaxies visible to him in his telescope were moving away from the Earth, supporting Lemaître's theory. In 1964, astronomer George Gamow theorized that there would be universal residual microwave background radiation if it were true that the universe had begun with a "big bang." In 1965, two scientists, Arno Penzias and Robert Wilson, accidentally proved him correct. As with many scientific discoveries, they were not looking to prove Gamow's theory. They were searching the skies for radio signals from space, but their efforts were constantly thwarted by background noise. Regardless of the direction they pointed their equipment, that noise was ever-present. That sound proved to be the cosmic microwave background radiation that had come from the original expansion of the universe, the Big Bang. This continuous sound, in the key of B flat, can be likened to the humming of a refrigerator: one is not consciously aware of the hum until the motor turns off. In the same way, we are not normally aware of this constant cosmic background noise, this sound of "Om," this sound of ShalOM-wholeness. But if it were to be turned off, we would notice it by the presence of its absence. Interestingly, of the many descriptive names people have for God, one is, "The Presence of an Absence."

"In the beginning there was the Word and the Word was with God, and the Word was God" (John 1:1). God thought, spoke, and breathed the Word of creation at once: in one motion, and then again and again, over and over, thought to word to action to creation, from imagination to realization. "And Wisdom (answering to the names *Hochma* and *Sophia*) was present with God at the beginning, in the creating, and in Wisdom were the hidden designs of God." And through Wisdom we will become closer to God. When God breathed and created with the Word, it was in the doing that He revealed Himself to us. And it is in our doing, our obeying, as co-creators with God that we come to know God and hear His clarion call, for we are like the ministering angels, "mighty warriors who fulfill His commands, attentive to the sound of His words"(Psalm 103:20).

The Word spoken by the One known as I Was, I Am, I Will Be, the first sound, like the spark that ignited the first burst of energy out of the darkness of the primeval black hole of nothingness, that expanded and became the universe, continues from alpha to omega, from yesterday to infinity. "In the beginning" began with the Word, the *Logos*, and the Mystery of Incarnation, and like the initial blast of energy that generated outward and forward into time, the Word continually informs creation through ideas, thoughts, beliefs, and behaviors. And that energy, like the divine spark placed in us by God, continues to live within each of us today, connecting us one to the other, to creation, to the past and the future.

> *I cannot think that the world, as we see it, is the result of chance; and yet I cannot look at each separate thing as the result of design.*
>
> —Charles Darwin

IV

"THE SNAKE TEMPTED ME"
(GENESIS 3)

The business of the philosopher is well done if
he succeeds in raising genuine doubts.
—Morris Raphael

I grew up in the city of Toronto. My mother and father met in Toronto during World War II. Toronto, Canada's largest city, was at that time mostly white, mostly Christian, and very much tied to England. It was the very essence of WASP: White Anglo-Saxon Protestant!

My mother told me stories about racism when she was growing up in Toronto. Anti-Semitic and anti-Irish sentiments abounded here in the 1920s and 1930s. Signs posted in public places warned against the admission of Jews, dogs, and Irishmen. Clubs were "Gentiles Only." Employment policies froze out Jewish applicants. Universities and professions imposed quotas on Jews. Jewish companies were boycotted. Toronto's anti-Semitism was deeply entrenched and out in the open.

My mother was an excellent executive assistant, but she had trouble finding employment because she was Jewish. So, on the advice of her high school teacher, my mother changed the pronunciation of her surname to give it a French or Christian flare. She also legally changed her first name from Sarah to Susan.

Canada was neither accommodating to nor tolerant of Jews already living in Canada. And it became even more difficult for Jews to immigrate to Canada after Adolf Hitler came to power in Germany, because Canadians' negative attitudes toward Jews still did not improve. My mother worked in offices where derogatory remarks about Jews were as common as tea and crumpets. She feigned illness around the Jewish holidays so that she could be home with the family and celebrate her traditions and beliefs. It required a great deal of finesse to pull this off every year. Perhaps the saving grace was that most non-Jews had no idea when our Jewish holidays occurred.

By the time I was in my teens and early twenties, Toronto had entered its teenage years as well. Experimenting with new ideas. Rebelling against the establishment. Toronto was opening its doors to more immigrants, especially from non-white countries. I didn't pay much attention to the changes. They seeped slowly into my consciousness. My children went to school and studied with children from many different races and cultures. The government went to great lengths to teach in favor of inclusiveness and against hate, racism, and bigotry. This was the cultural soup that washed over us. Different ethnic groups, different foods, and different traditions were just there, like the sun.

When I was fifty-eight, I moved to a small, very White Christian hamlet near a very White and Christian community. I remember walking down the streets of that little town and thinking that I was the odd one. Everyone was so "white." There are four churches on one block of this five-block town. No mosques, no Hindu Temples, no Chinese temples . . . and no synagogues, for that matter. As odd as it sounds, to me this was culture shock. I was accustomed to many colors, many styles of clothing, and many accents. I had moved from multi-ethnic to uni-cultural. And that makes Christmastime wonderful.

At Christmas, the whole town is dressed up, which reminds me of the early days in Toronto when my parents took us downtown to see the Christmas windows at the major department stores. In this town, people still say "Merry Christmas!" in public and in stores—something that is frowned upon in multicultural Toronto. I love the feel of this community, held together by its shared experiences, beliefs, and stories.

So I was taken aback when I observed an incident that seemed to me to be anti-Christian. I realized that political correctness, which has evolved along with immigration, had taken hold even in this rural Christian community. Somewhere along the way to inclusion, accommodation, and tolerance, it became acceptable for the politically correct, secular, agnostic, atheistic Left to demean and denigrate and disrespect those of us who believe in the Bible and the ethical values it teaches. In response, others took up the sword of righteousness and turned religion into Religionism. The rest of us have sat by the river and wept.

While people of other cultures and beliefs have moved to Canada to share in the benefits of our Western society, we have behaved like very good hosts who do not want to offend our guests—even after they have moved into our house and rearranged the furniture. Every other culture is wonderful and exotic, we are told, while ours is considered so familiar that it evokes contempt.

> *Every other culture is wonderful and exotic, we are told, while ours is considered so familiar that it evokes contempt.*

In response to this incoming tide of new cultures and ethnicities and this politically correct assault on our Judeo-Christian values, some people are tempted to respond with fear.

But we forget that fear opens the gate to authoritarianism. God's admonition against fear is a major theme of the Bible. God and His prophets constantly preach against fear, because fear is an emotional rather than a rational response to an event. When people are emotional, others can lead them down a dark path in the name of enlightenment. Yet here we are, going through a period of economic and cultural upheaval, and we are responding with fear.

Our response is similar to Europe's response in the last three decades of the nineteenth century, which was also a time of economic upheaval and increasing rural-to-urban migration. Then, too, there was a sense of angst and despair and fear of the future. New philosophies attempted to counteract the "profound sense of loss, a sense that a spiritual connection with nature and the cosmos had been sacrificed"[26] on the altar of industrialization. These philosophies "exalted myth over history, impulsive action or deed over conscious reflection, and feeling or intuition over rational

26 Richard Noll, *The Aryan Christ: The Secret Life of Carl Jung*, 115.

thought."[27] Romanticism, which was a desire to re-engage with innocence, spread throughout Europe, especially in the newly united Germany. Jungian psychology was questioning monotheism, turning instead towards the mystery cults of antiquity that Jung believed would free people from the repressive mask of civility imposed on them by monotheism, which he thought alienated them from their natural roots, their connection to the instinctive and intuitive natural man.[28]

These ideologies resonate again today. Some of us are holding tighter to the Bible, taking the words literally, both historically and scientifically. Many others are turning to new spiritual leaders, who are, once again, questioning the religion of ethical monotheism, the ties that bind us one to the other and to God, telling us that religion is preventing us from connecting to the true spirit and to our true selves. They tell us, once again, that monotheism is the enemy, while the intuitive man of feelings is the hero.

I came crashing up against these New Age philosophies at a volunteer training program for a local hospice.

I have always had a desire, or maybe it's a compulsion, to fix things, especially people. I have suggestions to make all kinds of situations better. When I was a young girl, I played the Blue Fairy in a class production of Pinocchio, so I had the thrill of sprinkling fairy dust and making magic. For me, this was type casting. That desire to fix, to smooth the way, led me to hospital chaplaincy when I was in my forties. After raising three children, I returned to university to study human behavior. My children probably would have received greater benefit if I had learned the subject before birthing them!

After I completed an undergraduate degree in Interdisciplinary Studies, majoring in human behavior, I found myself on a beach on Long Island, New York, talking with friends, when suddenly I knew what I wanted to do with my life. It came over me out of the blue. Actually it didn't so much come over me as it filled me. I sensed something like air or wind filling me up. Imagine taking in a deep,

---

[27] Ibid.
[28] Ibid., 143.

endless breath that lifts you up, higher and higher, while everything below you becomes clearer and clearer. I have been told that what I experienced was "being filled with the Spirit," the *Ruach*, of God. I knew then that I wanted to work with people in crisis, but not within the rubric of the psycho-social sciences. I knew that I wanted to help people from a religious perspective. When I returned home I discovered a program, clinical pastoral education, that is taught in hospitals. I already had the prerequisites, and so began my studies in chaplaincy.

Many people wonder why I chose this path, to stand beside people who face serious health crises and even death. I stand beside families making difficult medical decisions about loved ones. I advocate for patients. I help them feel the presence of God, and this helps them share pain and sorrow with me in a way that is different from sharing their feelings and fears with medical professionals. And, to me, that is the most rewarding of gifts to have been given.

I was looking forward to working as a hospital chaplain but life, unfortunately, got in the way of living. Have you ever worked toward a goal, anticipating the fruits of your labor, when suddenly all went awry? That is life getting in the way of living. For the next ten years, any hope of working as a chaplain slipped way, and not so gently. My physical and mental health were suddenly in jeopardy. (I'll share the details later.)

In 2010, the planets realigned, so to speak. I had moved to a place I call the Garden of Eden. My mental and physical health had returned. There was a new hospice opening in my little community. They were looking for volunteers. I met with the coordinators of the program and told them I was a multi-faith-endorsed, hospital-trained chaplain. I gave them my credentials and my letters of reference and told them I would be happy to be their volunteer chaplain. I lived nearby and was willing to come to the hospice any time of day or night. They seemed thrilled.

I would have to participate in a 30-hour program for volunteers in order to qualify, but I looked forward to the opportunity. The majority of the volunteers were women and most of them volunteered because they had personally experienced a health crisis or had cared for a loved one who had died. They wanted to use their experiences to help others. The topics covered in the program were all familiar to me, but I believe there is always an opportunity to learn something new in every situation. I was especially looking forward to the section on "Religion and Spirituality." Hospice care requires the ability to care for people from differing cultures and with diverse belief systems; as a multi-faith chaplain, this section truly appealed to me.

In the program sessions we usually just discussed the topic of the day, but one day I walked into the room to find the chairs set up in a circle around a small table in the center, on which sat a candle and a box of Kleenex. For this session we had two facilitators. The lead facilitator, a tall, middle-aged gentleman with a deep and comforting voice, asked us to take a seat. He invited us to place our feet firmly on the ground, to "ground ourselves." He then led us in a series of breathing exercises to prepare us to meditate. Meditating and deep breathing had been introduced earlier by our other facilitator, a lovely woman who reminded me of the women of the Sixties, with long hair braided down her back almost to her waist; she wore the long flowing skirts and tops that always evoke in me the image of an "Earth mother." Then the man turned on some music similar to the music played in my yoga and Pilates classes, asked us to close our eyes, and he read to us from the poetry of Rumi, a Persian religious mystic.

During the three-hour session we talked about feelings, and then we shared our feelings about photographs that had been provided by the instructors. We participated in an exercise in which we wrote down character traits such as love, charity, and empathy, and then had to prioritize them in an order in which we would be prepared to give them up. Religion was mentioned only twice. Once, when we were directed to handouts where we found a list of religions and some points about each religion. The second time, Ruth, a participant, asked a question about Jesus. The male facilitator's response was "Oh, yes, thousands of years ago there was this mysterious event, and . . ." His voice dropped away and, with a gesture of his hand, a turn of his wrist, . . . he indicated that there was no more to be said.

We did not talk at all about prayer or various religious rituals or symbols. We did not discuss spirituality from a Judeo-Christian perspective. At the end of the three-hour session, the male facilitator came around to each of us with an urn-like jug that was filled with stones, from which we each took a token of the afternoon. I'm not sure what I was supposed to do with this stone; I had no idea what it was supposed to mean. I know that many religious people have stones that have meaning for them, such as a rosary, or worry beads. In Judaism, people place stones on the monuments of their loved ones when they visit the cemetery. But this stone that was offered to me had no meaning at all.

I was quite surprised by the lack of religious and spiritual content in the sessions. Actually, I was shocked. We had been provided with a handbook that included a section on "Spiritual Issues at End of Life." This section included summaries of Buddhism, Christianity, Hinduism, Islam, Judaism, and Sikhism. It provided guidelines for spiritual conversations, such as "Do you consider yourself part of an organized religion?" "Do you belong to a religious or spiritual community?" "Do you believe in God?" "Do you pray or meditate, read scripture, attend religious services, listen to music, commune with nature?" Hospice volunteers are to provide this type of spiritual support by first respecting the beliefs of the client and their family members. We are admonished against sharing our personal beliefs unless asked, and most important, we are told never to proselytize or try to convert a client or family member. There is no "one size fits all" approach. But in this program, we never discussed different approaches based on different belief systems.

We didn't talk about those who believe in God: whether the God of the Christians and Jews and the fact that among Christians and Jews there are differences in prayers, symbols and rituals, nor about the beliefs of those who believe in many gods.

I remember once being called to the maternity ward. Whenever I received a call like that—with no reason given—my stomach would clench; I feared the worst. This time, a lovely young woman had given birth to a beautiful baby girl. She wanted me to prepare a ceremony welcoming her daughter into the community and expressing gratitude for her safe arrival. I was unfamiliar with her religious beliefs. We talked a bit and I offered to bring in a Spiritual Care provider from her religious background as many people are more comfortable speaking to someone from their own religious background. No, she said. I was to invoke my God in the prayers because she was open to all gods! To provide Spiritual Care for the many, we must learn about the beliefs of others and, at the very least, be respectful of their way of connecting with their God.

V

COME, LET US REASON TOGETHER
(ISAIAH 1:18)

I do not feel obliged to believe that the same God who has endowed us with sense, reason, and intellect has intended us to forgo their use.

—Galileo Galilei,
in a letter to the
Grand Duchess Christina

I could not understand how, in a seminar on how to be a compassionate and competent chaplain, we could possibly discuss religion and spirituality without discussing God and monotheism—especially in our little community. How did God and monotheism become passé and politically incorrect, while deep breathing and meditating on the poetry of Rumi, a thirteenth-century-Persian, Muslim, Sufi mystic poet, become the gateway to one's soul? When did reciting Rumi become a replacement for or an improvement on prayer? How did the poetry of Rumi become an alternative to Psalm 23 of King David, "Yahweh is my Shepherd, I shall not want," or the verse from Psalm 22 attributed to Jesus on the cross: "My God, my God, why have you forsaken me?" How do we talk about spirituality without the language of the soul: words like forgiveness, repentance, grace, sacredness, and gratitude? When did the music of Eastern religions and practices, such as yoga, usurp ecclesiastical music from Gregorian chant to Handel's *Messiah*, Mozart, Beethoven, and Leonard Cohen?

So I asked the male facilitator about his background. I have been taught by people from many faith backgrounds, but I could not discern his. He had returned to school as an adult and had chosen to obtain his divinity degree in Wisdom Spirituality from Wisdom University, an online university. This university provides graduate degrees that "honor the integrity and uniqueness of each and every student." One of its aims is to "catalyze the spiritual and personal transformation" of its students so that they can become more authentic selves. A major portion of each day in Wisdom Spirituality is spent on "transformational art," which includes developing intuitive and artistic expressions through mask-making and drumming. Our facilitator was actually *proud* that his studies in spirituality excluded all aspects of monotheism! But his concept of spirituality was totally foreign to me. It was, I suppose, meant to be an inclusive, ephemeral spirituality, all feeling-based. And then I learned that the school from which he had received his degree has no standing in any country and no national government acknowledges his credentials. Now I truly was at a loss.

It appears that Wisdom University is catering to an emerging cultural group, "Cultural Creatives," for whom there are "dramatic and urgent political, religious, economic and social implications for both the existence of this group and the values they hold." Dr. Paul Ray is the director of the Institute for the Emerging Wisdom Culture that is taught as Wisdom University. The institute promotes the belief that we are living in a time of duress. "Economic disruption, ecological instability, social alienation, our political incompetence are converging to produce an almost universal sense of unease about whether our systems of government can maintain any sense of institutional normalcy or moral integrity."

Dr. Ray describes these Cultural Creatives as representing a "dramatic departure from the traditional value system of religious fundamentalists." He describes them as "the emerging wisdom culture." Dr. Ray writes that "the old world is indeed dying but not as some think, at the hands of an angry God. The old is dying because something newer, more fundamentally humane, is arising in its place. This is the emerging wisdom culture."[29] This is the culture of that facilitator. He brought these beliefs into the room when he should have left them at the door.

This philosophy that Dr. Ray espouses is not new. It is a disturbing echo from the past. Go back and reread my paragraphs

---

[29] "The Institute on Emerging Wisdom Culture," Wisdom University website, http://www.wisdomuniversity.org/emerging-culture.htm.

about early-twentieth-century Europe's fear of the future, the rise of Romanticism, and the backlash against God and religion for alienating us from nature. The Age of the Enlightenment (the Age of Reason) in eighteenth-century Europe changed the way of thinking of the newly educated elite. For centuries, people had lived on the land at the mercy of nature; but Western Europe was modernizing. The culture was moving beyond the constraints of nature, from a pastoral culture to industrial. And with this shift came a change in the understanding of God. Just as we were no longer so strongly bound to the earth and the perfidies of nature, now, it was thought, we no longer needed an immutable and divine God.[30]

Those were heady times: progress was the new idol, and reason, science, and art were undermining religion. Rationalist philosophers pursued an "objective" reality of God. Hume, Descartes, Voltaire, Locke, Diderot, Mendelssohn, and Kant questioned the traditional beliefs and prejudices of the time, especially those of religion, and emphasized the primacy of reason and the strict scientific method. Voltaire proclaimed that the decline in religion would reduce hatred, fanaticism, and savagery. "With the decline in the strength of religious creeds . . . there would follow a concomitant decline in human hatreds, in the urge to destroy another man" because of his religious beliefs. Over time, people would become indifferent to religion and this indifference would lead to tolerance.[31]

There was a pursuit of a new, rational human being rather than one who simply believed. Deism made its debut and was followed by atheism. According to the Marquis de Condorcet of France (1743–1794), man was infinitely capable of perfecting himself without the assistance of a deity.[32] The Scottish philosopher David Hume believed that reality can be explained by science and there was no philosophical reason to believe in anything that could not be physically experienced.[33] Paul Heinrich Dietrich, Baron d'Holbach, wrote in the early nineteenth century: "If the ignorance of nations gave birth to the Gods, the knowledge of nature is

[30] Karen Armstrong, A History of God, 295.
[31] George Steiner, In Bluebeard's Castle, 47.
[32] Max Dimont, Jews, God, and History, 310.
[33] Armstrong, God, 341.

calculated to destroy them."[34] By the late-nineteenth and early-twentieth century, the theories of Freud, Nietzsche, and Marx were contemptuous of belief in God.

France and Germany were considered the most enlightened of countries in Europe. They were the leaders in science and reason. They were the hotbeds of philosophical discussions of theism, deism, and atheism. Nietzsche preached that there was "no ultimate meaning or value and human beings had no business offering an indulgent alternative in God."[35] He proclaimed the birth of a "Superman," an enlightened, psychologically powerful man who would declare war upon old Christian values. But instead of leading to the promised utopia, this constellation of beliefs—no ultimate meaning or value to life; man is capable of perfecting himself; a powerful Super-leader who is supposedly superior in intelligence to other mortals; the worship of science and the death of God—led to the greatest century of atrocities in human history. Worshiping science and human willpower while removing all moral restraints led to the pseudoscience of Nazi Germany, a country populated with intellectuals, philosophers, and scientists, a country steeped in the revelations of the Enlightenment.

> *Removing God from society gave governments free rein to manipulate the definition of "human," and those who did not fit the new definition were fodder for the furnaces along with all the other "trash."*

It was in this environment that governments were given free rein to manipulate the definition of "human," and those who did not fit the new definition were fodder for the furnaces along with all the other "trash."

So we should fear New Age philosophers and philosophies whose first act is to remove God from our culture. It is dangerous to throw away 3500 years of ethical monotheism, one God, and the Judeo-Christian ethic for a new round of Romanticism.

---

34 Ibid., 344.
35 Armstrong, *God*, 357.

It was quite clear that the Judeo-Christian ethic was anathema to the instructors of Wisdom Spirituality, though, so they decided for all of us that God need not be part of our discussion on religion and spirituality. A skewed view of inclusion and accommodation had taken hold. Belief in God was not included in the ideology of inclusiveness. Instead, the facilitators of the program imposed meditation, deep breathing, and shared feelings as the definition of spirituality. One size fits all. (Not only that, they made no effort even to teach us about the religions and traditions of patients who might access this facility, including First Peoples ("Native Americans") and those of the Muslim, Sikh, and Hindu faiths.)

If Moses, Rabbi Hillel, Jesus, or St. Augustine had been in my seminar, they would have been aghast; they would not recognize the meaning or purpose of "spirituality" as described by our modern spiritual gurus of the month. And they would be shocked by the lack of respect accorded to ethical monotheism and the Judeo-Christian ethic in twenty-first-century Western culture.

This was the point where I realized that I had taken for granted that the morals, values, and teachings of ethical monotheism would always be part of Western culture: especially here, in my small, rural village. And I am not alone. As a society, we inherited a magnificent gift from our ancestors but then put it in a drawer and forgot about it. The time has come to open the drawer, reclaim the gift, and polish it for the present time.

Almost forty years ago, philosopher George Steiner warned about being urged "to give up the proud image of *Homo sapiens*— man the knower, man the hunter of knowledge—and go over to that enchanting vision [of] *Homo ludens*, which means, quite simply, man the player of games, man the relaxed, the intuitive, the pastoral being."[36] There is a danger in this philosophy of "I feel, therefore I know," because it lacks the understanding of the importance of the need to acquire knowledge through critical thinking.

Religion and Spirituality are not meant to be understood only through feelings. They bloom in a climate of reason, rationality, and study. "By searching for truth with unrelenting zeal a man opens his

---

[36] Steiner, *Nostalgia*), 58.

soul to the flow of divine grace. So reason leads man's spirit to that which is beyond all human understanding."[37] The words in the Bible first speak to our minds and then touch our souls. I believe that ethical monotheism, the belief in one God and the Judeo-Christian ethic, a system of morals and values that have been practiced for more than 3500 years, must be reclaimed from the pastiche of these New Age philosophies if we are to continue to live in a democracy that remains open to all. Hermann Cohen taught that: "revelation is the creation of reason."

Needless to say, I was not invited to be a volunteer at the hospice. I was told that I would not understand the needs of the people in care. I wasn't properly grounded; in what, I don't know. I was at first shocked, hurt, then upset. I admit that I had been so excited about volunteering as the in-house chaplain it never occurred to me that I would not be accepted. There is a dearth of hospital-trained chaplains, especially ones who *want* to volunteer.

It seemed so odd that someone with my background would be turned away. Getting over my pride, I realized that I was angry that people with no respect at all for God would label me "inappropriate" to care for people in spiritual crisis; that I would not understand the patients' needs. These people seemed to believe that I might impose my views on God on the people in hospice care. Yet these were the same people who had just imposed their alien religious views on us. I had fallen down the rabbit hole. I realized that my small homogenous community was losing its connection to its religio-ethical heritage. I realized it was time to rediscover, reclaim, and nurture the culture that had been given to me, and to pass it on to those who follow.

---

[37] Agus, *Jewish Thought*, 173.

VI
AM I MY BROTHER'S KEEPER?

Without a love of humankind there is no love
of God.

—Sholem Asch, *from* What I Believe

Thousands of years ago, the Israelites wandered through the desert from Egypt, east to Jordan and then west into the Promised Land. It was a short journey that took forty years. God saw that His people were suffering from the fear of freedom. They were unable to cope. He knew that in order to go forward into the land of hope and promise, His people needed to taste freedom in the present so they could relinquish the slavery of the past, because memories of enslavement can drag us back into the past. But these lessons require time and effort. For the Israelites it took forty years, until all those who had been enslaved—physically, morally, intellectually, and spiritually—had died and the new generation—those not raised in slavery—were ready to move forward.

I know it is hard to understand why it would take any time at all to revel in freedom, let alone forty years. But freedom has to be learned. Think of people who are imprisoned for many years and are finally released. Imagine what it must be like for them. I remember the 1994 movie *The Shawshank Redemption*. We meet Andy Dufresne, who has been wrongly convicted of two murders and is sentenced to two consecutive life terms. In jail he befriends Ellis Boyd "Red" Redding and Brooks, who has been in jail for decades. Brooks is paroled after serving fifty years. He leaves jail, his home of fifty years. A place where he was told what to do, when and how, and was given everything he needed. We watch him as he exits the gates and see right away that he is uncomfortable. He is taken into town, given a place to stay—and is lost. Frightened, he doesn't know what to do. He can't manage the freedom that was suddenly bestowed upon him, so he hangs himself. When Red is finally paroled, he too, suffers from freedom. But he survives—

perhaps because there is a friend waiting for him to guide in his new world. "A prisoner cannot release himself from prison."[38] Like the Jews in the desert, Red required not only time, but guidance. For the Jewish people, that guidance came from the revelation of the moral laws passed down at Mount Sinai. These laws brought twelve tribes together, transferring loyalty from tribe to nation, with loyalty to the ethical system, a shared belief that bound them together. I doubt very much if they knew the crucial role they would play in history, if they understood the extraordinary unending revolution that they were bringing to the world. And yet that is the same ethical system from which Western society developed its morals and values:

> For I was hungry and you gave me food; I was thirsty and you gave me something to drink; I was a stranger and you welcomed me; I was naked and you gave me clothing; I was sick and you took care of me. I was in prison and you visited me. Matthew 25:35–36

The stories in the Bible promote the importance of caring for the other, a principle which is fundamental in a democracy. Adam and Eve were sent from the Garden and told to till the soil, and only by the sweat of their faces would they earn their food. Eve gave birth to Cain, and then to Abel. Abel became a shepherd, while Cain tilled the soil. Both the brothers brought offerings to God, and God showed a preference for the offering from Abel. This offended Cain. He took his brother for a walk in the open country . . . and killed him. Then God asked Cain, "Where is your brother?" And Cain lied. He said he didn't know. Perhaps it was dawning on him that ending his brother's life over a sacrifice was horribly wrong. How was he to know? Where would he have learned about the sanctity of life? And then Cain asked the crucial question: "Am I my brother's keeper?"

And so, within ninety lines of the story of creation, we are given the reason for the Bible. "Am I my brother's keeper?" is a leitmotif of the Bible. And the rest of this book contains God's ethical response to that question: Yes, you are your brother's keeper. You

---

[38] Berakhot 5b.

are your brother's keeper because all life is sacred. The murder of Abel by his brother Cain is to teach us that to kill another is to kill an entire world, just as to save another is to save the entire world.[39]

The Mosaic laws and the writings of the prophets constantly remind us of our obligations to others. In the beginning, these calls to care were directed at the Jewish people, the first people to embrace this ethical God. Then, through Israel, the teachings of this monotheistic, ethical God are made available to all.

> In that day, the root of Jesse, standing as a signal for the peoples, will be sought out by the nations and its home will be glorious. Isaiah 11:10

Isaiah offers the vision of universal peace:

> The mountain of Yahweh's house will rise higher than the mountains. . . . Then all the nations will stream to it, many peoples will come and say, "Come, let us go up to the mountain of Yahweh, to the house of the god of Jacob, that he may teach us his ways so that we walk in his paths." Isaiah 2:3

> And God said,

> "It is not enough for you to be my servant, to restore the tribes of Jacob and bring back the survivors of Israel;

> I shall make you a light unto the nations so that my salvation may reach the remotest parts of the earth." Isaiah 49:6

What started as a tribal belief moved to a belief that is universal. Isaiah continued the refinement of the ethic that brought us this new consciousness not built on selfishness. Isaiah is teaching us that our survival is only assured if we care for the other and not just our own needs, or the needs of our small clan.

Today there are still many people living in tribal cultures. Attempts have been made to reshape these into democratic societies; both from within and without (for example, in Iraq). We have great expectations for these societies; but our expectations are

---

[39] Arthur Hertzberg, *Judaism: The Unity of the Jewish Spirit Throughout the Ages*, 179.

unrealistic. After all, it required thousands of years for this cultural transformation to come to maturity in our Judeo-Christian societies. We humans, unfortunately, seem able only to develop freedom of self and then of community in small increments at a time; in slivers. People raised in autocratic and theocratic cultures are like the Israelites in the desert following their escape from Egypt. They may be physically free, but not necessarily psychically or emotionally ready to handle freedom and all the decisions that freedom requires. Ayaan Hirsi Ali, who grew up in Somalia and Kenya, wrote in her book *Nomad* about her experiences living in a tribal culture, and then the culture shock she experienced when she arrived in Holland as a refugee. "It was a journey from Africa, a place where people are members of a tribe, to Europe and America, where people are citizens . . . along the way I learned many lessons. I learned that it is one thing to say farewell to tribal life; it is quite another to practice the life of a citizen."[40]

> *"It is one thing to say farewell to tribal life; it is quite another to practice the life of a citizen [in the West]."*
>
> —Ayaan Hirsi Ali

It is the Judeo-Christian religio-ethic that provides the path to citizenship, because it privileges intrinsic human value (the foundation of security for a person) and free will, prerequisites for societies that value freedom. Freedom requires an ethical system that cannot be hijacked by any one person or ideology, whether secular or theological.

At Mount Sinai God said, "You shall not oppress the stranger; you know how a stranger feels, for you yourselves were once strangers in Egypt" (Exodus 23:9). The story of the Exodus of the Israelites from their enslavement in Egypt is well known. God, through the spirit of Moses, had His people released from Pharaoh, and they fled toward the desert and the Sea of Reeds (the Red Sea). But Pharaoh changed his mind and set out after them to capture them. God parted the sea, letting the Israelites pass on dry land and,

---

[40] Hirsi Ali, *Nomad*, xvi.

then, when the Egyptians were in the middle of the sea, God closed the waters and destroyed Pharaoh's army. The Israelites cheered and sang in honor of God. Miriam, Moses' sister, took up her tambourine, and all the women joined in the revelry.

There is a commentary in one of the many books about the Bible that imagines God's response to the happiness of the Israelites after the drowning of the Egyptians. God hears the angels singing and celebrating His great victory. But instead of rejoicing with them over the rescue of His people from enslavement, God weeps and rebukes them. "Why are you singing?" He asks. "Why are you rejoicing? The Egyptians are My children, too, and they are dead, drowned in the sea. There is no cause for you to sing. Their deaths are not to be celebrated."

Belief in a cruel God makes a cruel man.
—Thomas Paine

God does not rejoice in the death of anyone, not even the wicked.[41] "Belief in a cruel God makes a cruel man." We are not to take God's name in vain by killing or maiming in His name; remember, you were once a stranger in a strange land. This is the definition of empathy: knowing how another feels. And the prophets and the judges and then the apostles constantly preached the need to practice and internalize this ethical lifestyle based on social justice and prophetic law, so that care of the other and obligations to community would override our instinctual, natural, selfish responses.

No man is an island,
Entire of itself . . .
Any man's death diminishes me,
For I am involved in mankind.

John Donne[42]

---

41 Ezekiel 18:32; 33:11.
42 John Donne, in *Devotions upon Emergent Occasions*, 1623.

VII
"YOU CREATED MY INMOST SELF ...
A WONDER AM I"
(PSALMS 139:13)

If I am not for myself, who will be for me?
And if I am only for myself, what am I?
And if not now, when?

—Rabbi Hillel

Western philosophy has developed a bad odor, many of our intellectuals have decreed. So in the name of "authenticity," we are being directed to other "more authentic" locations. Religious fundamentalists on the Right, so closed-minded that nothing new can get in, and atheistic/agnostic/secular ideologues on the Left, so open-minded that their brains fall out, have become the modern incarnation of the serpent in the Garden of Eden.

Western culture is being stifled in the middle. It is chic to look for oneself in Eastern meditative philosophies and religions and foreign cultures, as if all the answers were there. But looking for one's authentic self in a foreign worldview is like trying to find your missing keys in a place you never visited. What is the "self," anyway? What does it mean to be authentic? What is an "authentic self?" Historian Huston Smith asks, "What is the secret of the 'I' with which one has been on such intimate terms all these years yet which remains a stranger? . . . What lurks behind the world's facade, animating it, ordering it-to what end?"[43]

What is the self? We cannot see it. We cannot touch it. It is not corporeal. We can lose parts of our body but the self will still be there in its entirety. Many sociologists, biologists, and philosophers have defined and described the self. Buddha defined the self (*anatta*) as "things perceived by all of the senses including the mind, but as

---

[43] Houston Smith, *The Religions of Man*, 64.

they are merely perceptions they should not be considered as things that can be owned or embraced by the self."

Looking for one's authentic self in a foreign worldview is like trying to find your missing keys in a place you never visited.

Jean-Jacques Rousseau pondered the self and its relationship with society. He chose the way of "feeling" to learn about the secrets of the self. He learned about his self through "reverie, the dream, the old memory, a stream of associations unhampered by rational control."[44] Socrates, by contrast, found the true nature of the self through reason, thinking, and discussion. To Socrates, "authenticity" was a vague criterion for distinguishing a healthy self. Allan Bloom described the difference between Rousseau and Socrates as "Socrates talking to two young men about the best regime, with the image of Rousseau, lying on his back on a raft floating on a gently undulating lake, sensing his existence."[45]

In the twentieth century, sociologist George Herbert Mead envisioned the self consisting of two parts: the "I," the core that is creative, spontaneous, yet unknowable, and the "me," which is the social self, the image we have developed of ourselves through interactions with others. Erving Goffman's theory of "dramaturgy" is similar to Mead's in that there is a part of the self that is unknowable. What we do reveal are different faces that depend on time, place, and circumstance. It is reminiscent of Shakespeare's concept of self from *As You Like It*: "All the world's a stage, and all the men and women merely players. They have their exits and their entrances, and one man in his time plays many parts."

Erik Erikson (1902–1994), a developmental psychologist and psychoanalyst, referred to the self as "the core" of a person's being. We are learning from neuroscientists like Dr. Antonio Damasio, a professor at the University of Southern California, that humans, unlike animals, are aware of their own bodies, their own "self," and

---

[44] Bloom, *Mind*, 179.
[45] Ibid.

this is the root of consciousness. To be conscious is to be open to the Self, the universe, and one's own unique self in the universe.

Allan Bloom described the essence of the self as "mysterious, ineffable, indefinable, unlimited, creative, known only by its deeds; in short, like God, of whom it is the impious mirror image."[46] There is a part of God that is concealed from us, a part that He would not share even with Moses. He insisted that Moses turn his face away when He moved past him. Perhaps we will come to know God and our authentic selves when the unknowable part of us, the divine spark, placed within us by this unknowable God, comes face to face with its Creator.

The dictionary defines authentic as "genuine, true, and reliable." To be authentic, one must be true to one's beliefs, values, and goals and then behave according to those beliefs, values, and goals. This raises the primary question: Upon what does one base one's beliefs, values, and goals? In the West, for millennia, this basis has been ethical monotheism as revealed in the Hebrew Bible and the Gospels; Judaism and Christianity.

> *Ethical monotheism brought about the greatest change in the collective unconscious of humanity since the caveman made fire.*

Ethical monotheism brought about the greatest change in the collective unconscious of humanity since the caveman made fire. Pantheism and paganism had kept us in bondage to the whims of nature with constant sacrifices to the gods, and never allowed us to believe that we had any control over our lives. Time was cyclical rather than linear, and we lived our lives like hamsters in a wheel. There was no sense of history or the idea that each moment has a meaning and or that we are all part of a long journey that has a beginning and will have a middle and an end: historical time, in other words, not the time of the seasons of nature.

And then came Abraham, and God calling out to him: "Come with me. Trust me."

---

[46] Bloom, *Mind*, 173.

And Abraham followed this ineffable, unknowable, ethereal God who told him that we humans have control over our lives. We are still connected to the Earth as are all living things, but more is expected of us. This loving, caring, compassionate God demands moral and ethical behavior from us. Social justice and prophetic law obligate us to care for the weakest in society, the hungry, the poor, the sick, the widow and orphan. And that we bury the dead. Among the obligations listed in a book written thousands of years ago, burying the dead is so important as to be specifically mentioned in social justice. Think of the implications. Think of the sacredness it places on human life.

> For this law which I am laying down for you today is neither obscure for you nor beyond your reach. It is not in heaven, so that you need not wonder, "Who will go up to heaven for us and bring it down to us, so that we can hear and practice it?" Nor is it beyond the seas, so that you need wonder, "Who will cross the sea for us and bring it back to us, so that we can hear and practice it?" No, the word is near to you, it is in your mouth and in your heart for you to put into practice. Deuteronomy 30:11–14

The Hebrew Bible and the Gospels, Judaism and Christianity, provide moral absolutes that are the line in the sand, the bar to which we all can aspire, while others around us define right from wrong based solely on their own wants and feelings. It was Machiavelli who decreed that selfishness is somehow good. Now, in the twenty-first century, we have prophets of selfishness teaching us that the good man is not the one who cares for others; rather, today's "good" man is the one who knows how to care for himself.[47]

These prophets encourage us to define our authentic selves by the wants of the heart rather than the needs of the head. This is an immature and Manichaean response to serious ethical dilemmas. This response foolishly assumes that a compassionate, empathic, civil society does not require that each citizen put forth the effort to deliberately constrain their innate self-centeredness. But there are

---

[47] Bloom, *Mind*, 178.

many times in life when we must sublimate our wants for the needs of others. In 1946, Lutheran pastor Martin Niemöller (1892–1984) wrote this famous poem that speaks to the absence of an authentic self:

> First they came for the communists,
> and I did not speak out—
> because I was not a communist; . . .
> Then they came for the trade unionists,
> and I did not speak out—
> because I was not a trade unionist;
> Then they came for the Jews,
> and I did not speak out—
> because I was not a Jew;
> Then they came for me—
> and there was no one left to speak out for me.[48]

And this brings us back to Rabbi Hillel and authenticity. The authentic self does not concern itself solely with its wants ("If I am not for myself") to the exclusion of the needs of others ("if I am only for myself"). We must define our values in order to begin the journey. Choosing to believe in one God, one accepts the obligations laid down in social justice and prophetic law. Moral and cultural relativism do not fit into this paradigm. Moral relativism lacks the universal principles and absolutes that are needed to guide one's behavior. Without absolutes, each culture can have its own "truths". Cultural relativists do not compare or contrast behaviors between cultures because, to them, behavior is considered right or wrong within its own culture. What are we to do, then, when we are faced with behavior in other cultures that we consider morally repugnant? How do we respond to behavior like ethnic cleansing, human trafficking, or flogging, or stoning women to death? Can we condone child brides, or young children forced to work in dank factories for barely subsistence wages?

Are we to accept these behaviors because these behaviors are accepted in those cultures? Or do we judge that behavior and say

---

[48] "Martin Niemöller," WikiQuote.org, accessed on November 20, 2014, http://en.wikiquote.org/wiki/Martin_Niemöller.

no to it? If we stand up and say no, then we have made an absolute moral judgement. How do we reconcile relativism with the knowledge that some behavior must never be tolerated? We can't. If you "find" your "authentic" self in a system with no hierarchy of morals, values, and ethics, no obligations or concomitant civic responsibilities, then you will never be authentic.

The modern quest for the authentic self focuses on personal feelings, a turning inward for answers, at the expense of outward behavior—our responsibility and obligation to others, to society. There is reluctance, especially in post-religion spirituality, for rules, for cultural or religious external constraints on the self.

I believe that "authenticity" has become a popular secular word in our secular world because it allows us to feel not guilty for being selfish. To be "authentic," today, means to be true to oneself, to prioritize one's needs and the wants of the perpetual subject, "I." But this modern concept of being true to oneself affects relationships within a community. If everyone in a community decides to be true to their own individual self, what becomes of the common good? What defines the common good? Who defines the common good? The "common" good will cease to exist, drowned in the flood of millions of individual "goods."

This is because, although democracy exists in order to allow people to *pursue* (within agreed-upon limits) their individual goods, the foundation of any viable democracy is, first of all, an agreement about the proper and permitted means to pursue and achieve our individual goods. In other words, a viable democracy must be based on a living *social contract*: what the philosophers Thomas Hobbes, John Locke, and Jean-Jacques Rousseau described as an agreement that makes it possible for citizens to "give up *certain* of their rights and freedoms, handing them over to a central authority, which in return, will ensure the rule of law within the society and the defense of the realm against external enemies."[49]

If, instead, everyone in a democracy only pursues their own individual goods and in any fashion they want to, then the social

---

[49] Rabbi Jonathan Sacks, Ebor Lectures 2011, presented at York St. John University, York, England, November 30, 2011, http://www.rabbisacks.org/biblical-insights-into-the-good-society-ebor-lecture-2012/.

contract—that invisible social infrastructure that protects our democracy and freedom and equality for all—will unravel, and our democracy will come crashing down. The twentieth century, that century of human horrors, should have taught us that when we lose sight of moral absolutes, whoever has power will define the "common" good after their own wishes, and then impose their good on others: think Stalin, Mao, Hitler, Pol Pot, and Kim Jong-il.

> *It is ethical monotheism that teaches us that more is expected of us than simply pursuing our individual rights and happiness.*

It is ethical monotheism that questions the unbounded, "natural," authentic self and finds it wanting. It is ethical monotheism that teaches us that more is expected of us than simply pursuing our individual rights and happiness. True authenticity comes from binding ourselves, like Abraham binding his son Isaac, to something beyond ourselves: to God and His teachings. As His children, created in His image, we have responsibilities, obligations, and duties to others, and we must think beyond our own wants and needs and instead act with empathy and compassion.

VIII

A Light unto the Nations: Ethical Monotheism and the Judeo-Christian Ethic

---

"There were peals of thunder and flashes of lightning dense cloud on the mountain and a very loud trumpet blast" (Exodus 19:16). We are all there together to "Hear, O Israel," to listen to the mighty Word from the heart of the fire, through the sound of trumpets of rolling thunder piercing the soul, circumcising the heart: a gift wrapped in mystery and heralded in awe.

—Author

In 1940, in the early stages of World War II, it took Germany a mere six weeks to conquer France. For two years afterward, France was divided between the northern occupied half and Vichy France in the south. Thousands of Jews who lived or made their way to the south survived in relative peace for two years. About 5000 Jews, mostly children, made their way to a small Protestant town, Le Chambon-sur-lignon, located in the mountains 350 miles south of Paris. In 1942, the Germans went into southern France and began to round up the Jews to send them to concentration camps, where they would be murdered.

There were approximately 5000 residents in the village of Le Chambon-sur-lignon. They were proud descendants of the first French Protestants, the Huguenots, who had been persecuted by the French government of King Louis XIV for their religious beliefs. The village, which became known as "that nest of Jews in Protestant Country," was also a place of convalescence for German soldiers. In other words, the locals' next-door neighbors were

Nazis.[50] Yet the families of Le Chambon-sur-lignon still sheltered every Jew who came to their village. They did this knowing full well that they were defying the French government, which was collaborating with the Nazis. The villagers provided the Jewish refugees with food, education, forged identification papers, and they also escorted many to Switzerland and freedom.

When you read this story, can you see yourself in it? Do you see yourself sheltering someone for whom you will be killed if they are discovered? Think about it. You have no connection to these people. They were never your neighbors. You didn't interact with them, or share food or holidays. They were complete strangers to whom you owed nothing. Can you envision yourself putting not only yourself in danger to save these strangers, but also putting in danger your children and anyone else living under your roof? Do you see yourself as someone who could keep this deed a secret, even from your next-door neighbor? Would you deprive your own children of food in order to feed strangers in your midst?

Now, add to this the culture in which the residents of Vichy France lived. They were well aware of the German attitude toward the Jews. In the Germany of those years, the "Jewish conspiracy" had been the explanation for everything that had gone wrong in the world. Jews were described as an alien people who endangered German citizens. Anti-Semitic propaganda was everywhere. Hatred of Jews was in the water and the air. In October 1940, Marshall Petain, chief of state of Vichy France, decreed that foreign Jews were to be rounded up and interned in special camps. Local government prefects could send Jews to concentration camps for any reason at all.

If you lived in such a place, could you rise above the culture in which you lived? How would you accomplish that? What would be your guiding force?

I have often asked myself if I would put myself in danger like that? I like to think that I would shelter a stranger in need of protection. I am not so sure that I would have the courage to

---

[50] "Le Chambon-Sur-Lignon," International Raoul Wallenberg Foundation, http://www.raoulwallenberg.net/ saviors/others/le-chambon-sur-lignon/.

shelter others if it meant putting my children in harm's way. I would like to think that I would. I would like to think of myself as that kind of person. But I think my first instinct would be to save myself and my family.

But the residents of Le Chambon-sur-lignon did not hesitate in their actions. They refused to round up the Jews and turn them over to the authorities. They behaved like Shifra and Puah, the Egyptian midwives who refused to follow the orders of the Pharaoh to murder the Hebrew male children (1: 17). The residents of Le Chambon-sur-lignon followed in the footsteps of "two of the great heroines of world literature, the first to teach humanity the moral limits of power . . . because [that power] was immoral, unethical, inhuman."[51]

Were those noble Frenchmen and French women and children just born that way? Did they come out of the womb filled with the milk of human kindness, willing and able to put the needs of others ahead of their own, like a wolf stopping in the woods to care for a wounded deer? Are we born generous and good, as Rousseau and the Enlightenment philosophers thought? Or do we come into the world with Original Sin? Are we neither kind nor unkind? Is "the tendency of man's heart is towards evil from his youth" (Genesis 8:21), so we teach kindness to be on the safe side? Experts in the fields of philosophy, biology, neurology, sociology, psychology, and anthropology have all weighed in on the definition of human nature. Some believe that we are born a *tabula rasa*, a blank slate upon which others (culture) create a story, while some believe that most of the story is already finished (genetics) before we take our first breath.

If it were true that we come into this world "good," all of us would behave like the villagers in Le Chambon-sur-lignon. But we don't. It's wishful thinking to tell ourselves otherwise. Philosopher Will Durant wrote, "The trouble with most people is that they think with their hopes or fears or wishes rather than their minds."

---

[51] Rabbi Jonathan Sacks, "On Not Obeying Immoral Orders," Covenant & Conversation, January 6, 2015, RabbiSacks.org, http:// www.rabbisacks.org/ obeying-immoral-orders-shemot-5775/.

The Bible describes what happens to our family, tribe, and nation when we allow ourselves to follow our own nature. The first family had a hellish start: fratricide. Cain killed his own brother. Abraham misled the pharaoh into believing that Sarah was his sister, not his wife, in order to spare his own life. Lot's daughters gave birth to children conceived by their father. Jacob, his mother's favorite, stole Esau's birthright and later was tricked into marrying Leah when he had asked for Rachel. Joseph's brothers threw him into a pit before selling him into slavery; they were jealous of him because he was their father's favorite. These are stories of unbridled human nature.

What if Immanuel Kant's teaching that "human nature is understood to be composed of selfish natural appetites"[52] is true? Then what? What if our primal survival instinct of selfishness is never replaced with care for others?

Consider babies. They look adorable, especially just a few days after birth when they look up at you, trying to focus their eyes on you. Yet they turn into screaming magpies in short order. If their needs are not met instantly, they start to complain; then the complaining gets noisier and the whining begins. If that doesn't get our attention, they scrunch up their little faces, their eyes become so small they almost disappear, and they beat their little fists in the air and scream so hard that you think they will stop breathing. It doesn't take long for our progeny to learn that the one who grabs attention is the one who has the best chance of survival. Selfishness is ingrained in us so that we can live and pass our genes down to the next generation. It is Darwinian. Why would we assume that selfish babies will become unselfish, sympathetic, empathic adults all by themselves? Logically, why should people care for others?

"There is a universal moral core that all humans share. The seeds of our understanding of justice, our understanding of right and wrong, are part of our biological nature. [Yet] we are predisposed to break the world up into different human groups based on the most subtle and seemingly irrelevant cues, and that, to some extent, is the dark side of morality . . . to some extent, a bias to favor the self,

---

52 Allan Bloom, Mind, 162.

where the self could be people who look like me, people who act like me, people who have the same taste as me, is a very strong human bias. It's what one would expect from a creature like us who evolved from natural selection, but it has terrible consequences."[53]

Evolution predisposes us to be wary of "the other" for survival, so we need society and parental nurturing to intervene. "And the truth is, when we're under pressure, when life is difficult, we regress to our younger selves and all of this elaborate stuff we have on top disappears."[54]

There are references throughout the Bible that call us to care for "the other." The prophet Isaiah expounds upon the importance of caring for others. He teaches and preaches the need to care for them, to rise above our personal survival and be concerned for the survival of people beyond our own tribe; he has to teach this because we are tribal from birth. The lesson of the Bible is neither myth nor magic—it is "the recognition of how small we are in the scheme of things, and how great is our responsibility to others."[55]

The lesson of the Bible is "the recognition of how small we are in the scheme of things, and how great is our responsibility to others."

—Rabbi Jonathan Sacks

We start in a family, the smallest unit of authority, and come together to form tribes, thus transferring our loyalty to tribal leaders. With time and the development of cities and city-states and ultimately to countries, loyalty has to move up the chain to the leaders of each new, larger unit. For loyalty to be maintained there must be commonly shared stories, commonly shared beliefs, desires, and goals. What keeps disparate tribes together if they cannot find commonality? We have seen what happens in countries like Pakistan, Afghanistan, Rwanda, Sudan, and Iraq. Left to our own instincts, we fall back onto our primal fear of the other and do

[53] Paul Bloom, professor of psychology at Yale University, in 2012 released studies from the Baby Lab that reveal the moral nature of babies from the age of three months.
[54] "Babies Help Unlock the Origins of Morality," CBS's *60 Minutes*, November 18, 2012.
[55] Rabbi Jonathan Sacks, "Challenging the Idols of the Secular Age," June 15, 2013, http://www.rabbisacks.org/challenging-the-idols-of-the-secular-age-credo/.

not care for the stranger.

Alexis de Tocqueville (1805–1859) pointed out that, even in democracies, "each citizen is habitually busy with the contemplation of a very petty object, which is himself."[56] Hobbes, Locke, and Rousseau all believed that men, in the state of nature, are free and equal and have all the rights to life, liberty, and the pursuit of property, but this state of nature is so often what leads men to war. Civil society's purpose is to protect each of us, one from the other, and "make peace where nature's imperfection causes war."[57]

Our inability to see beyond tribal loyalties is surely one of nature's worst imperfections. Yet here we are in the twenty-first century, where so many people wax nostalgic over the past, yearning to return to times when we were "closer to nature" and our natural roots. This urge to romanticize the past comes from deep within our being.

The myth of Prometheus tells the story of our deep desire to become one with nature again. Prometheus stole fire from Zeus and brought it to mankind. He suffered terribly for that theft. With this gift, man is no longer solely under the control of the gods and the whim of nature. With fire, he can cook his food. He can light up the night and he can warm himself and live without fear of freezing to death, unlike the animals, which are still rooted only in nature and natural law. With the advent of fire, we have one foot in the world of nature and one foot in the world of human nature. Fire comes to represent "man's cultural break with the natural world, and the deep discomforts which this break has left in our souls."[58] For those of us who believe in God, that break causes our longing to return to the Source. For those who don't, it leads many to romanticize nature.

Straddling these two worlds requires a balancing act: between our animal instincts that drive us to take what we want when we want it, and the knowledge that we can now control our environment and modify our behavior. Animals act on their

---

[56] Allan Bloom, *Mind*, 86.
[57] Allan Bloom, *Mind*, 162–3.
[58] Steiner, *Nostalgia*, 29.

instincts. They go with the flow without concern for their actions. They are doers without guilt or shame because for them there is no such thing as right or wrong. A lion gives chase to a zebra and pounces on it, tearing into its flesh, because the lion is hungry and the zebra is there for the taking. There is no concern for "the other." There is no sense of remorse.

This break with nature leaves us with a feeling of unease, anxiety, and angst. Questions and answers become much more complex, because we have moved beyond the animal kingdom's instinctive responses. There is a constant battle between our natural desires, which we hold in common with the animal world, and our human moral responses. This battle takes place in the gap between instinct and action, where free will holds reign. "He himself made human beings in the beginning, and then left them free to make their own decisions."[59] Human nature requires laws or morals because human free will, the ability to control our response to those instincts and drives, needs direction.

It was the great Dutch philosopher Spinoza who wrote that there is a difference between natural and moral order. From Spinoza's *Tractatus Politicus* (1676): "The law and ordinance of nature under which all men are born, and for the most part live, forbids nothing but what no one wishes or is able to do and is not opposed to strife, hatred, anger, treachery, or in general anything that appetite suggests."[60] Organized societies require moral order because "there is no altruism among nations. . . . Since fear of solitude exists on all men, because no one in solitude is strong enough to defend himself and procure the necessaries of life, it follows that men by nature turn towards social organization . . . . Men are not born for citizenship, but must be made fit for it."[61]

Freud wrote in 1928 that if not for religion there would be mayhem: "If one imagined its prohibitions removed, then one could choose any woman who took one's fancy as one's sexual object, one could kill without hesitation one's rival or whoever interfered with one in any other way, and one could seize what one

---

[59] Ben Sira, *Ecclesiasticus* 15:14.
[60] Durant, *Philosophy*, 209.
[61] Ibid.

wanted of another man's goods without asking his leave."[62] Freud was not religious, but he knew the importance of the ethical teachings. "If you want to expel religion from our European civilization, you can only do it by means of another system of doctrines."[63]

> *Organized societies require moral order because "there is no altruism among nations."*
>
> —Will Durant

We come from the animal kingdom, and animals live within a system of hierarchies that bring order to potential chaos. It is instinctual. The male lion keeps order in the pride. Alpha males fight over who will be the leader. As Freud wrote, we too need controls and doctrines. Back to Spinoza: "Men are not by nature equipped for mutual forbearance of social order."[64] I suggest that at this time, the best form of hierarchy is ethical monotheism, the "miracle" that brings selfish genes together to produce selfless people.

Religion based merely on ritual or symbols is not enough to soothe our inner turmoil. It is the ethical underpinnings that help us to make the difficult decisions, the decisions that go against our instinctual passion: passions which are stronger than reasonable interests or the interests of the others in our family or community or nation.

Morals given in the name of God give us pause when our natural selfish desires come calling. Human laws can too easily be put aside. We have seen this far too often in recent memory: from the Armenian genocide to the Nazis; from Pol Pot in Cambodia to the Hutus in Rwanda, and now the massacres in Nigeria by Boko Haram, and by ISIS of Muslims and Christians in the Middle East.

There are two absolute moral responses to events; one is saying "yes," the other is saying "no." We rarely think about the importance of the "moral no," what the late Sir Isaiah Berlin spoke

---

[62] Ferguson, *Civilization*, 271–2.
[63] Ibid.
[64] Durant, 209.

of as "positive liberty": the freedom to do what one ought, which can often compete with negative liberty, which is the freedom to do what one likes. This 'moral no" is unique to human beings. It is the ability to say no to something that may be legal, but that is morally and ethically wrong. We lived through a moral collapse in the first decade of this century when the greed of the few made it possible for some to get exceptionally wealthy at the expense of those less fortunate and less worldly. Those with power took advantage of those without. Rare was the one who spoke up. Rare was the one who knew the moral meaning of free will, which includes saying no to a practice that would harm the many while prospering the few. Refusing to act is one-half of the equation in exercising free will. We have this ability to choose because we are swaddled and bathed in freedom, from birth until the day our dust returns to dust. That freedom comes from the ethical system we follow: our rules of living together. Will those rules benefit the few or the many?

IX
WHAT OUGHT I DO?

I call heaven and earth to record this day against you, that I have set before you life and death, blessing and cursing: therefore choose life, that both thou and thy seed may live.

Deuteronomy 30:19

Ethics is the system of values we choose to help us make moral decisions that answer the question, "What ought I do?" How we answer that question goes to the very soul of our society, because ultimately "the test of the humanity of a human being is the degree to which he is sensitive to other people's suffering."[65] There are many ethical systems and many different ways to categorize them. I am dividing them into two broad categories: the ethics of entitlement and the ethics of rights and responsibilities.

Andre Trocmé, the pastor in Le Chambon-sur-lignon, followed an ethic of rights and responsibilities: the Judeo-Christian ethic. He led his flock by example, taking Jews into his home and protecting the stranger, just as his ancestors had been protected by their neighbors from religious persecution. The citizens of Le Chambon-sur-lignon had no legal obligation to protect the Jews in their midst. Rather, they felt it was their duty to help people in need and did not consider their actions as heroic or dangerous. Where did this selfless sense of duty come from? It came from an ethical system that promoted specific duties, responsibilities, and obligations.

"Right actions that spring from forethought are of greater worth than those that are involuntary."[66] The citizens of Le Chambon-sur-lignon read and believed the moral teachings of the stories in the Bible; they followed ethical monotheism and the Judeo-Christian

---

[65] Abraham Joshua Heschel, *The Insecurity of Freedom*, 252.
[66] Agus, *Jewish Thought*, 92.

ethic. The revolutionary teachings about caring for the stranger, the weak, the widow and orphan were part of their cultural DNA, their understanding of being human. Oxford University biologist Richard Dawkins describes two types of information that are intertwined and passed through the generations. There are the genes that pass on our DNA, and then there are *memes*, which he refers to as "units of deep cultural information."[67] The Judeo-Christian memes, these "deep units of cultural information," were embedded in the residents of Le Chambon-sur-lignon because they had been passed down through the millennia.

In 1940, when Great Britain was threatened with invasion by Nazi Germany, Mahatma Gandhi called out to the British:

> *I appeal for cessation of hostilities . . . because war is bad in essence. You want to kill Nazism. Your soldiers are doing the same work of destruction as the Germans. The only difference is that perhaps yours are not as thorough as the Germans . . . I venture to present you with a nobler and a braver way, worthy of the bravest soldiers. I want you to fight Nazism without arms or . . . with non-violent arms. I would like you to lay down the arms you have as being useless for saving you or humanity. You will invite Herr Hitler and Signor Mussolini to take what they want of the countries you call your possessions. Let them take possession of your beautiful island, with your many beautiful buildings. You will give all these but neither your souls, nor your minds. If these gentlemen choose to occupy your homes, you will vacate them. If they do not give you free passage out, you will allow yourself, man, woman and child, to be slaughtered, but you will refuse to owe allegiance to them . . . I am telling His Excellency the Viceroy that my services are at the disposal of His Majesty's Government, should they consider them of any practical use in advancing the object of my appeal.*

Mahatma Gandhi practiced Hinduism all his life. His ethic rejected the "doctrine of the sword." Hinduism's central teaching is

---

[67] Somerville, The Ethical Imagination, 98.

that the mercy of kindness is the essence of all religion. Gandhi followed the teachings of the Hindu philosopher Tulsidas: "Good and bad, all men are the creation of god. The man of god picks up the good and discards the bad like the proverbial swan which is able to drink the milk and leave behind the water, when the mixture of water and milk is placed before it."[68]

The question we are left to answer is the definition of good and bad. I was raised in the Judeo-Christian ethic which "leads me down paths of righteousness" when I want to run and hide, and offers me shelter "in its still waters" when I am afraid (Psalm 23). Gandhi's answer, his ethical priority, seems to be to walk away from evil. This is an ethic that was unknown to the people of Le Chambon-sur-lignon.

When Moses stumbled upon a bush ablaze with fire while not being consumed, he stopped in wonderment. And then he heard a voice. It was the voice of the God of Abraham, Isaac, and Jacob. Moses covered his face, afraid to look; he was afraid of the unknown. Isaiah tells us, "Do not be afraid, for I am with you" (Isaiah 41:10). He tells us that God is with us so that we can overcome our fears, because fear endangers freedom and free will.

St. Thomas Aquinas wrote, "Fear is such a powerful emotion for humans that when we allow it to take us over, it drives compassion right out of our hearts." Fear opens the door to the dirges and lamentations of false prophets tempting us into the arms of false messiahs, whether they are politically correct secularists or Biblical fundamentalists. Religion, the teachings of this moral God, is a bastion against the siren call of fear-mongering barbarians. This God demanded of us that we have no other gods before Him, that we not bow down to other gods or serve them. If we continue to place God in the center of our lives, there will be no room for idols to worship, from material goods to the latest religious or political hero.

Fear tempts us into the arms of false messiahs, whether they are politically correct secularists or

---

[68] Mahatma Gandhi, "Mahatma Gandhi on Hinduism," Gitananda.org, http://www.gitananda.org/ hinduism/mahatma-gandhi-on-hinduism.html/.

Biblical fundamentalists.

In the story of creation, God created us and placed us above the gnat and just below the angels to remind us that we come from the natural world, that we are related to all living things, great and small. But by placing us below the angels, He is telling us that more is expected of us than merely existing or being. The Judeo-Christian ethic as taught to us by the God of Abraham, Isaac, Jacob, and Jesus teaches us to rise above ourselves, to reach for the Seraphim, the highest order of God's angels; to live a moral and ethical life that comes with responsibilities, duties, and obligations to others that provide for dignity for all. Paul, in his letter to the Philippians, says it simply and beautifully:

> *Whatever is true, whatever is honorable, whatever is just, whatever is pure, whatever is lovely, whatever is gracious, if there is any excellence, if there is anything worthy of praise, think about these things.* Philippians 4:8

Approximately 2000 years before Jesus walked the earth, a family headed by a man named Terah left its home in the city of Ur in Babylonia (now modern Iraq), to make its way to Canaan, but they stopped in Haran (southeastern Turkey). In Terah's time, people lived in tribal communities tied together through family. Here is Abram, son of Terah, walking among his flocks, caring for his wife Sarai, when a voice calls out to him. *Go forth*, the voice says. *Leave your home and I will take you to a new place and make a great nation of you.* So Abram gathers his family and off they go to Canaan (Judea).

What was Abraham thinking? First, he was listening to a voice who claimed to be God. His tribe already prayed to their own gods and had idols made in their image. Before God introduced Himself to Abram, the population prayed to multiple gods with names like Marduk, Baal, and Anat, and female goddesses such as Ashera, Ishtar, and Isis; the people believed that these gods interacted with them, flowing in and out of their lives without rhyme or reason and implementing natural disasters at whim. There was a sense of defeatism, as if the people had no control over their lives, that nothing they could do would change their lot in life. And they sacrificed their children to the gods, like Moloch of Canaan, in hopes of making their lives better.

Yet Abram chose to listen to the voice and follow it; he took a leap of action. With that fearless leap, Abram was transformed. And his name reflects that transformation. He will now be known as Abraham. Imagine, today, leaving your home, your friends, your place of worship, your belief in your gods, and going to a new place, an unknown place, to start a new life because a voice called out to you. And taking your family with you, away from everything that gave them a sense of security and comfort. Imagine believing in only one God after having been taught to believe in many. Could you?

So began the story and history of ethical monotheism that surrounds us today. From this one family, the belief in one God developed: not only one God, but a God who taught His people ethics and morals and made demands of their nation, the first of His followers, that no other god or gods before had ever done. We know this one God by many names, including Yahweh, Adonai, and Elohim. The religion is Judaism.

Irish author Thomas Cahill wrote, "The Jews gave us the Outside and the Inside—our outlook and our inner life. We dream Jewish dreams and hope Jewish hopes. Most of our best words, in fact—*new, adventure, surprise; unique, individual, person, vocation; time, history, future, freedom, spirit, faith, hope, justice*—are gifts of the Jews."[69]

What is so beautiful about these teachings is that God intentionally revealed them in the desert, in the wilderness, publicly and openly, in a place to which no one had any claim. "Everyone who desires to accept, let him come and accept."[70] Ethical monotheism freed us from the belief that we had no control over our destiny, that we were mere pieces in the games of capricious gods. Aristotle, in his *Magna Moralia* ("Great Ethics"), wrote that the stars—the gods, as the ancients thought—had control over "the external goods" of man such as friends and family and appearance, but not over intellectual and moral virtues, which he called "goods of the soul."[71] From the moment that Adam and Eve ate of the forbidden fruit, we have been exhorted to choose—because we

---

[69] Cahill, The Gifts of the Jews, 261.
[70] Mekhilta, Bahodesh 1.
[71] Ross King, *Machiavelli*, 62.

have been blessed with the responsibility to exercise free will. We can choose to be active participants in our own lives or we can choose to be victims. The choice we make will affect the way we live out our lives and the way we interact with others.

Ethical monotheism taught us that we each have intrinsic value—*we matter because we exist*; we are valued for who we are, not for what we do or for our financial worth. And this new knowledge, that we matter because we exist, changes our way of treating others, because we are forced to see others as equals. We are *all* wanted and loved by this ethical God.

There is no way of moving directly from tyranny to a free society. I remember the glory days of the Arab Spring; everyone was on an emotional high. I wasn't so optimistic. Look, they said, change is in the wind. Sadly, that's exactly where the change existed—only in the wind. The rhetoric was exalting, but democracy does not blossom rapidly and spontaneously just because the seed is planted. And attempting to plant that seed in a culture based on submission can raise expectations too high for success.

Freedom does not come easily. Rather, it must be taught in the culture.[72]

We learned this from the Biblical story of the Exodus. Forty years passed in the desert before the Jews were allowed entry into the Promised Land, because they had to be ready to look forward with hope rather than backward from fear. They had to internalize a new way of living.

The belief in an ethical God makes it possible, over time, to move from a society of tribes to a society of many tribes held together with commonly shared beliefs, stories, and traditions, because this God demands that we care for the other, the stranger, because we know how a stranger feels; we were once strangers in a strange land (see Exodus 23:9). At first we were welcomed by the stranger, the Egyptian, who took us in during a famine and treated

72 Essay, "What's Gone Wrong with Democracy," *The Economist*, http://www.economist.com/ news/ essays/ 21596796- democracy- was- most- successful- political- idea- 20th- century- why- has- it- run- trouble- and- what- can- be- do

us as if we were of their tribe. It was only later that they enslaved us.

This commandment to care for others seems so simple, so natural. Yet still today, there are countries where tribal warfare is the norm. Within one country, two tribes often cannot find enough shared experiences or beliefs or stories to unite them. They are like the lion and the lamb. Here in the West we aspire to live peacefully with people of different colors, beliefs, ethnicities, and cultures. But we had to learn this behavior; it did not come naturally. It has been passed down to us over the millennia. We haven't always succeeded in following the commandment. But that is a *human* failure and not a failure of the religio-ethic that teaches it.

> *This commandment to care for others seems so simple, so natural. Yet still today, there are countries where tribal warfare is the norm.*

Millennia ago, as time passed and new cultures formed, a pantheon of gods connected with natural phenomena and human emotions such as love, hate, and jealousy came and went. Zeus, Aphrodite, Dionysus, Persephone, and Eros were among the most prominent Greek gods. They were known for their animosity and cruelty toward one another and even toward the people who worshiped them. When the Romans overwhelmed the Greeks, they incorporated the Greek gods into their culture, changed the names to Jupiter, Venus, Bacchus, Proserpina, and Cupid, and continued to live as if these gods lived right next door. In a sense, they did. Temples to the gods were strewn throughout the cities. Citizens brought sacrifices to these temples as well as money for the priests to appease the gods who acted out of self-interest, just like their subjects. Yet ethical monotheism continued to survive.

At the turn of the Common Era, 2,000 years ago, Jerusalem, in the land of Judea, was the center of Judaism, and the Temple Mount was its hub. Commerce took place at the Temple, but more importantly, the Sanhedrin (the court of justice) gathered there and disseminated the laws of God, as given at Mount Sinai and interpreted over the years by the prophets, the judges, and then the rabbis. Over time, though, divisions arose among the Jews regarding the interpretation and the fulfillment of these laws.

Around one hundred years prior, about 100 BCE (Before the Common Era), Rome was involved in wars against a new empire, Parthia, on their eastern front, so Rome decided to take their stand in heavily fortified Judea. To pay for the defenses, the Romans taxed the Jews to the point of rebellion. The Jews in the area known as the Galilee became disenchanted with their Roman rulers[73] and they rebelled against them. At the same time, the Jews were involved in internecine quarrels amongst themselves. Some complained about the Sadducees, that they paid too much attention to ritual. Then there were the Essenes, who separated themselves from the rest of the Jewish community and followed a more pious lifestyle, one that included celibacy. In the middle position resided the Pharisees, the most tolerant of the sects: they followed the path of leniency in religious rulings and were more open to interpretation to fit the changing times. Into this mix came a new view of honoring God, based on inner piety, from a branch of the Essenes.

In the third decade of the Common Era, the preaching of a young rabbi known as Yeshua, Jesus, from the Galilee, brought new converts to Judaism by teaching and preaching this change in focus and stressing the "prophetic core of Judaism: the passion for justice, the reverence for humility, the unwavering advocacy of ways of gentleness, kindness, and peace."[74] After his death, the Apostle Paul preached far and wide about this man called Christ. This new sect, which came to be known as Christianity, espoused the morals, values, and ethics of the Jews as revealed by the God of Abraham, Isaac, and Jacob to the greater Gentile population around the Mediterranean Sea. Christianity was at first a combination of Greek theology and Jewish morality.[75]

The Hebrew Bible, filled with these teachings, the Gospels, and the New Testament make up the backbone of the Judeo-Christian ethic as practiced today in the Western world.

[73] Dimont, Jews, God, and History, 90–94.
[74] Agus, Jewish Thought, 302.
[75] Durant, Philosophy, 543.

The development of Western civilization is about the slow translation of the teachings of ethical monotheism into institutions, social structures, and ethical codes. Biblical Judaism made no room for feudalism, social hierarchy, chauvinistic nationalism, caste spirit, or privileged classes.[76] Rather, it taught the laws of ethical monotheism: rules by which to live in a compassionate society. In order to become closer to God, the people needed to follow His laws. *Behavior mattered.* The prophets preached the importance of internalizing these laws by "circumcising" one's heart with them. Jesus, a rabbi, also preached the importance of the laws.

> *Do not imagine that I have come to abolish the Law or the Prophets. I have come not to abolish but to complete them. In truth I tell you, till heaven and earth disappear, not one [dot], not one [stroke of the pen], is to disappear from the Law until all its purpose is achieved.*

> Matthew 5:17–18

But more than that, Jesus wanted his flock of followers to love the spirit of the law as much as the letter of the law. Jesus wanted the people to learn that their thoughts and feelings played a role in their behavior. It isn't enough to do what you are told; you have to internalize it so that it becomes a part of your soul. And that, to me, is the definition of faith.

Why is it important to know the origins and meaning of ethical monotheism? Because here, in the Western world, Judeo-Christian ethical monotheism is fundamentally related to Western civilization and society.

In 1991, Pope John Paul II explained the importance of the Judeo-Christian ethic:

> *Those who are convinced that they know the truth and firmly adhere to it are considered unreliable from a democratic point of view, since they do not accept that truth is subject to variation according to different political trends. It must be observed in this regard that if there is no ultimate truth to guide and direct political activity, then ideas and*

---

[76] Wistrich, *Betrayal*, 98.

convictions can easily be manipulated for reasons of power.
As history demonstrates, a democracy without values easily
turns into open or thinly disguised totalitarianism.[77]

This ethic has survived through the millennia while other cultures and religions have faded away. The Judeo-Christian ethic, the Hebrew Bible and the Gospels, are with us today because they have bequeathed to us a culture that prioritizes freedom, justice, and the fullness of human dignity, because each person, each man or woman, rich or poor, powerful or powerless, is the image of God and is therefore of immense, nonnegotiable, unquantifiable value. We are each equally made in the image of God, therefore we stand as equals in the presence of God. Our Judeo-Christian culture has bequeathed to us our knowledge of free will that requires us to balance rights and responsibilities with compassion, the rule of law with the attitudes of mercy and love.

Unfortunately, like fish in the sea, we have taken our life-giving, life-sustaining surroundings for granted, and now the ideologies of secularism, agnosticism, atheism, and political correctness have been elevated to the status of Champions of Objective Truth that will somehow protect us from intolerance, war, and all the other human evils that these interest groups wrongly blame on every religion.

Our culture will only survive if ethical monotheism and the Judeo-Christian ethic are taught. And one does not need to be Jewish or Christian to value a culture that is informed by these teachings.

Too many of us no longer know or understand the meaning of ethical monotheism and the Judeo-Christian ethic and how it has so fantastically transformed humanity. We no longer teach these concepts in school, even though they are the foundation of our society. It is as if we assume that our children will learn about their culture through osmosis. They won't. Our culture will only survive

[77] Father Raymond J. de Souza, "God, Truth and the Free Society," May 2011, http://fatherdesouza.ca/?page_id=661.

if ethical monotheism and the Judeo-Christian ethic are taught. And one does not need to be Jewish or Christian to value a culture that is informed by these teachings.

The New Testament says, "No one who relies on this will be brought to disgrace, it makes no distinction between Jew and Greek: the same Lord is the Lord of all and His generosity is offered to all who appeal to Him, for all who call on the name of the Lord will be saved" (Romans 10:11).

Isaiah offers a vision of universal peace: "The mountain of Yahweh's house will rise higher than the mountains . . . . Then all the nations will stream to it, many peoples will come and say, 'Come, let us go up to the mountain of Yahweh, to the house of the God of Jacob that he may teach us his ways so that we walk in his paths" (Isaiah 2:3).

And Micah 4:5: "For let all people walk everyone in the name of his god, and we will walk in the name of the Lord our God for ever and ever."

Winston Churchill wrote that the Bible has given us "a system of ethics which, even if it were entirely separated from the supernatural, would be incomparably the most precious possession of mankind, worth in fact the fruits of all other wisdom and learning put together. On that system and by that faith there has been built out of the wreck of the Roman Empire the whole of our existing civilization."[78]

Sigmund Freud, the father of psychoanalysis, described culture as "the sum of the achievements and institutions which differentiate our lives from those of our animal forebears and serve two purposes, namely that of protecting humanity against nature and of regulating the relations of human beings among themselves."[79]

The Judeo-Christian ethic colors every aspect of Western culture, including the basic principles of our social, political, and judicial systems. It is the foundation of our lifestyle. Our secular

---

[78] Martin Gilbert, *Churchill and the Jews*, 38.
[79] *The Wisdom of Freud* (New York: Philosophical Library, 1950), 18.

system of justice comes to us from the time of Moses and the Israelites in the desert. Freedom is so vital to our evolution that God Himself taught us by example—by His hand He freed the Israelites from their enslavement to Pharaoh and, by extension, He freed all peoples from all pharaohs.

> *The Judeo-Christian ethic colors every aspect of Western culture, including the basic principles of our social, political, and judicial systems. It is the foundation of our lifestyle.*

It was Moses's father-in-law, Jethro, who said that Moses could not be the judge for all the people. Moses would be the teacher of the laws and statutes given by God, but dispensing justice required a group of trustworthy and incorruptible group of men. The law would be brought closer to the people by judges of "heads of thousands, hundreds, fifties and tens" (Exodus 18:21). These judges would deal with minor cases in law and refer the more serious cases to Moses. It is the paradigm today for our national, provincial, state, and local courts: power is shared, and it is not in the hands of only one man.

The Bible is a book of laws that have become the foundation of Western government and justice. From out of the wilderness, a new form of nation emerged. New laws were decreed to make living together possible. There were laws about the legal rights of women, ownership of land, the waging of war, and the design of courts. Leviticus 5:1 decrees that one must offer testimony if one has important information; Leviticus 5:21–23 says one must return property taken dishonestly; Leviticus 10:8–11 says a priest may not enter the sanctuary or render a legal ruling while intoxicated; Leviticus 18:21 is the prohibition against sacrificing children; Leviticus 19:10 contains prohibitions against greed—one must leave a portion of one's harvest for the poor; Leviticus 19:11 prohibits stealing.

There are prohibitions against delaying payment to a day laborer and against judges who may favor the rich over the poor. And then there is the obligation to defend victims of violence, as one is not allowed to stand by while another's blood is shed. There are admonitions against giving false evidence (perjury), and requirements that more than one witness is mandated to convict someone of a crime (Deuteronomy 19: 15–16). "If you have resident aliens in your country, you will not molest them. You will treat resident aliens as though they were native-born and love them as yourself, for you were once aliens in Egypt" (Leviticus 19:33–4). There are laws about safe building practices (Deuteronomy 22:8). There are laws about business: "You must not keep two different weights in your bag, one heavy, one light. You must not keep two different measures in your house, one large, one small. You must keep one weight, full and accurate" (Deuteronomy 25:13–15).

The commandment regarding the Sabbath requires rest for the family, the domestic help, and also the cattle. There are laws regarding the care of animals, because animals are not things. They have a soul, so they are to be protected. There is a commandment to treat them with kindness. And the Bible teaches empathy regarding animals: do not take a mother bird with her young; do not take the chicks in the presence of the mother bird.

And if ethical monotheism has this much concern for animals, imagine the concern it has for humans!

So a new nation walked out of the desert and into the Promised Land. It brought with it a new ethic that prioritized justice, peace, and caring for the weak and the oppressed, and protecting them from the strong and wealthy.

Yahweh says this:
Let the sage not boast of wisdom,
Nor the valiant of valour
Nor the wealthy of riches.
But let anyone who wants to boast of this:
Of understanding and knowing Me.
For I am Yahweh, who act with faithful love ,
Justice, and uprightness on earth;
Yes, these are what please Me,
Yahweh declares.

Jeremiah 9:22–23

X
WHAT DOES IT MEAN TO BE HUMAN?

PART 1:
ETHICS OF RESPONSIBILITIES, OBLIGATIONS, AND DUTIES

Never mind your happiness; do your duty.
—Will Durant

Many years ago, when I represented the chaplaincy department of my hospital on the obstetrics/gynecology ethics committee, we were presented with the case of a woman who had received assistance to become pregnant. An ultrasound revealed that two fetuses had implanted. She decided that she only wanted one child. Years later I was visiting a hospital when I saw two young people come out of the office of a doctor who specialized in heart conditions in the fetus. The young woman came out the door, placed her back against the wall, and slowly crumpled to the ground. The young man walked away from her, down the hall, head in hands, stifling a primal, guttural scream. Having cared for families making decisions about abortion due to genetic problems, I knew what had taken place in that office. Painful decisions had been thrust upon this young couple.

How does a potential parent make decisions about a pregnancy? This question ultimately forces us to ask, "What does it mean to be human?" The culturally accepted definition of "human" speaks to the soul of a society. Will you choose as your baseline an ethic that begins with the idea that all life intrinsically has absolute value, that the meaning of human is not negotiable? Or will you choose an ethic that makes it possible to redefine the meaning of human?

Biologically, we know that human beings start with a fertilized egg, called a *zygote*. In just forty-six successive divisions, the single cell that contained one double set of genes, one set from the man and one set from the woman, has grown to thirty-five trillion cells. The Catholic Church states that, from the moment of conception, the unborn child is considered a human being. In Jewish law an unborn fetus is not considered a person until it has been born, but "legal permissibility is not synonymous with moral license."[80] In other words, although a fetus is not a person legally, morally a fetus has potential life. The English obstetrician R.F.R. Gardner, a Christian, describes the fetus as "at least a potential and developing human being."[81] There are others who have a non-personal view of a fetus;[82] they don't see the fetus as having life. These are some of the views about life and when it begins.

Now it is up to each of us to decide which ethic best speaks to the society in which we live: the society we wish to bequeath to our children and all who will follow us. The Judeo-Christian ethic, the ethic of rights and responsibilities, defines a human being as a sacred child of God created in His image. "God created man in the image of himself . . . male and female he created them" (Genesis 1:27). Therefore, all human beings must be treated with dignity and respect. Human beings have an absolute intrinsic value; we matter because we exist, whether we are obese or beautiful; intelligent or developmentally challenged; mentally ill or a genius; exceptionally wealthy or homeless.

The former Chief Rabbi of Great Britain, Lord Sacks, wrote, "Collective nouns group things together; proper names distinguish them as individuals. Only what we value, do we name." As written in Psalm 147. "He counts the number of the stars and calls them each by name." A name is a marker of uniqueness.[83]

St. Paul considered it immoral to treat a human being as a thing rather than as a person to be loved.[84] Not only are we created in

---

[80] Fred Rosner, *Modern Medicine and Jewish Ethics*, 150.
[81] Joseph Fletcher, *The Ethics of Genetic Control*, 92 and 120.
[82] Ibid., 134.
[83] Rabbi Jonathan Sacks, "What Counts," Covenant & Conversation, *Aish.com*, May 12, 2013, http://www.aish.com/tp/i/sacks/207104401.html.
[84] John Shelby Spong, *Reclaiming the Bible for a Non-Religious World*, 250.

God's image, we carry within us the divine spark that connects us one to the other and to God. Immanuel Kant (1724–1804) developed an ethical system based on rational thinking, on pure practical reason, and he also concluded that people have an absolute intrinsic value. Kant wrote, "Act in such a way that you always treat humanity, whether in your own person or in the person of any other, never simply as a means, but always at the same time as an end."[85] This statement carries within it the same concept as the Golden Rule, "Do unto others as you would have them do unto you."

Kant's ethical system, like the ethics espoused in the Bible, demands respect for all humanity and that we "uphold the human rights of all persons, regardless of where they live or how well we know them, simply because they are human beings, capable of reason, and therefore worthy of respect."[86] It is a reiteration of God's command that we care for the stranger since we were once strangers in a strange land and that, yes, we are our brother's keeper.

Both ethical systems, religious and secular, espouse the sanctity of life. Both ethical systems are universally against murder and suicide. The sixth commandment, "Thou shall not murder," comes from God, and we follow the commandment because God said so. Kant would say that if it is good for one person to commit murder, it is good for all. If it is not good for one person to commit murder, it is not good for all. The admonition against murder is a *categorical imperative* because it is absolute and universal and true for all people all the time. The categorical imperative is absolute and universal in the same way that a commandment from God is absolute and universal.

Kant's ethical system also has a categorical imperative against suicide, because people have intrinsic value. You cannot use a human being for some ulterior motive or purpose, as merely a means to an end. Killing oneself is a means to an end: perhaps the means to end pain. Killing oneself is like murder: treating a person as a thing that can be disposed of and failing to respect humanity as

85 Michael J. Sandel, Justice: *What's the Right Thing to Do?*, 122.
86 Ibid., 123.

an end in itself. Another way of understanding Kant's position is to view suicide from the perspective of a categorical imperative. If suicide is good for one it is good for all. Suicide, like murder, is counterproductive for a society. Kant's ethical stance on suicide and murder mirrors the teaching in the Bible: "Today I call heaven and earth to witness against you: I am offering you life and death, blessing and curse. Choose life, then, so that you and your descendants may live" (Deuteronomy 30:19–20).

For Kant and the Judeo-Christian ethic, morals are absolute—objective, not subjective. In these two ethical systems, subjective feelings have no place in moral decision-making. The story of the Exodus pits God, through Moses, against Pharaoh. God wants Pharaoh to let His people go. And then God does something that seems to make no sense. God hardened Pharaoh's heart. Why would God harden the heart of this man? The great sages have come up with an explanation for God's actions. God wanted Pharaoh to base his decision on reason, not feelings. God wanted Pharaoh's response to be head-strong when letting His people go and not heart-felt. God did not want Pharaoh crying later that he let his emotions dictate his actions. God wanted Pharaoh to be rational, objective, in his deliberations.

For Kant, for an action to be morally good "it is not enough that it should *conform* to the moral law—it must also be done for the *sake* of the moral law. It is similar to the concept of following God's commandments because they come from God. For Kant, the motive that confers moral worth on an action is the motive of duty, by which Kant means doing the right thing for the right reason."[87]

Most people choose to live because they enjoy life; life has meaning and purpose. They live, not because of the categorical imperative to live or because God commands us to choose life. But for someone who has lost hope and wants to die, choosing to live, to overcome the desire to die, is an example of doing the right thing for the right reason: they choose to live because it is their duty to live in Kant's ethical system and it is an obligation in the Judeo-Christian ethic. I think this is one of the most difficult ethical

---

[87] Sandel, *Justice*, 111.

concepts to internalize and accept. We are to live because it is the right, or moral, thing to do; enjoying our life is not the issue. For Kant and for God, we should behave morally because it is our duty, our obligation to behave that way. For those of us who have faced the temptation to end our own lives, the obligation to live can be the difference between life and death.

Kantian secular ethics and religion-based Judeo-Christian ethics are similar in their expectations. They both begin with the statement that life is sacred. Yet I think it is far more difficult to live under a secular ethical system like Kant's than to live with the Judeo-Christian ethical system as the foundation of our culture. Human beings are imperfect. We are bound to fail morally. There is no mechanism for repentance and forgiveness in Kant's secular ethical system. The Judeo-Christian ethic is based on the knowledge that we are imperfect creatures, and it provides the path to forgiveness, redemption, and hopefulness, through ritual, symbol, tradition, and prayer.

XI
WHAT DOES IT MEAN TO BE HUMAN?

PART 2:
THE ETHICS OF ENTITLEMENT

Without ethical culture, there is no salvation for humanity.

—Albert Einstein[88]

Now we need to examine the ethics of entitlement. Jeremy Bentham (1748–1832), an English moral philosopher, conceived the doctrine of Utilitarianism, or Moral Relativism, sometimes referred to as Situational Ethics. Bentham taught that "the highest principle of morality is to maximize happiness, the overall balance of pleasure over pain."[89] Utilitarianism uses *feelings* as the arbiter of decision-making, both individually and universally. This ethical system gives priority to "whatever produces happiness and pleasure" over that which causes pain and sorrow.

John Stuart Mill (1806–1873), like Bentham, was also a proponent of Utilitarianism. He wrote that "the theory of life on which this theory of morality is grounded—(is) namely, that pleasure and freedom from pain are the only things desirable as ends; and that all desirable things . . . are desirable either for pleasure inherent in themselves or as means to the promotion of pleasure and the prevention of pain."[90]

This ethical system places almost no limits on an individual's moral or public behavior, and the only limits that can be placed must be decided by the individual alone. As long as one's actions

---
[88] https://sites.google.com/site/swanezine/ethics-and-morality-quotes.
[89] Sandel, *Justice*, 34.
[90] Sandel, 53.

do not bring harm to others, this ethic says, each of us has the right to do as we see fit. One's "independence is, of right, absolute. Over himself, over his own body and mind, the individual is sovereign."[91]

So what is the value of other human beings in Mill and Bentham's system? It is merely what happiness they can give to another; their only value is extrinsic, as judged by someone else. In other words, Utilitarianism (Moral Relativism) says that you have no intrinsic value simply because you are a living human being: you only have value if someone else decides that you can make them happy in some way.

In a community, the Utilitarian ethic of happiness is based on delivering the greatest good for the greatest number. But since this ethical system is based on an individual's subjective feelings, desires, wants, or preferences, it is impossible to develop universal moral laws, because feelings, desire, wants, and preferences are constantly changing, both personally and culturally. Happiness is not universal, it is personal; it is all about me.

And if "happiness" is the priority, then there is less need to think of long-term consequences, to be concerned for what will be after one dies. Happiness for one may be a big car and for another a large house. Since the basis of this ethical system is subjective, all preferences count equally, which makes it a non-judgemental system, unlike the Kantian or the Judeo-Christian ethic.

There is another ethical debate that belongs here: the sanctity-of-life ethic versus the quality-of-life ethic. Joseph Fletcher wrote in *The Ethics of Genetic Control,* "The world no longer needs all the individuals we are capable of bringing into it—especially those who are unable to compete and are an unhappy burden to others. If the size of our families must be limited, surely we are *entitled* to children who are healthy rather than defective."[92] In this view, the definition of *human* changes: now it is based merely on each individual's definition of healthy and defective. Brown eyes might be considered defective to one person. A girl might be considered defective to another. Then there are those who argue that "humans

---

92 Fletcher, *Ethics,* 85; italics mine.

are no different in any essential moral respect from other animals."[93] Once we take away anything sacred about human beings, it is so much easier to rid ourselves of those not acceptable to the ideal of our particular generation.

The beginning and end of life are fragile moments. Without a finite definition of human, we can choose to end a pregnancy because it is a girl and we want a boy, and we can rally around a parent's choice to end life because they seem to be unhappy.

I don't believe that morality based on happiness and individual rights makes us better or more compassionate. Yes, I am making a judgement here. I assume that a compassionate society is the best society. I fear Utilitarianism in all its forms because it is based on the greatest good for the greatest number. But who defines the greatest good? When the definition of good changes, then what? If ethics have no extrinsic or intrinsic substantive base, then ethical decisions will be made by those in power who can impose their beliefs on others.[94] What if the majority's definition of good tramples the needs of a minority?

An ethical system that lacks an absolute definition of what it means to be human is wide open to crimes against humanity. Under Joseph Stalin, millions of people were starved, many of them deliberately—they weren't worthy of life, he had decided; they didn't fit his vision. Mao Zedong destroyed the lives of millions of human beings when he radically reorganized society based on his personal vision, a vision that lacked any sense of compassion for those he forcefully exiled, imprisoned, and executed. People were merely a means to an end for Mao: and the end was his happiness, based on his opinion of the greatest good for the greatest number. In Rwanda, 1994, the Hutus carved up the Tutsis with machetes. This heinous act was made possible by teaching the Hutus that the Tutsis were vermin, not human. Yet it is almost impossible to distinguish a Tutsi from a Hutu. To know for certain, one must look at the person's papers to see the tribal designation. And then there is Hitler. His idea of the greatest good for the greatest number was to rid the world of Jews. He was able to murder six

---

[93] Somerville, *Imagination*, 65.
[94] Ibid., 85.

million Jews by spreading propaganda over many years that redefined Jews as vermin, rats, garbage. From there it was but a few steps to the incinerator.

Are we as a society better off since the rise of the ideologies of Jeremy Bentham? I think the rise in entitlement ethics is leaving us bereft of compassion and empathy. We are pulling away from any moral obligation to those with less, the weak, the infirm, and the different. Rabbi Jonathan Sacks writes, "If everyone is free to do what they like, the result will be freedom for the strong but not the weak, the rich but not the poor, the powerful but not the powerless. A free society requires restraint and the rule of law. There is such a thing as a constitution of liberty. That is what the Israelites acquired at Mount Sinai in the form of the covenant."[95]

[95] Rabbi Jonathan Sacks, as quoted by Yitzhak on his blog ‏ויב יד וידי, "Only the Servant of God is Free," April 18, 2010, http:// bdld.info/ 2010/04/18/ only-the-servant-of-god-is-free-on-various-conceptions-of-liberty/.

XII
DO YOU CHOOSE LIFE FOR YOU AND YOUR DESCENDANTS?

"We're all human, aren't we?
Every human life is worth the same,
and worth saving."

—J.K. Rowling,
Harry Potter and the Deathly Hallows

Now it is time to return to the two cases regarding abortion: the woman implanted with two fetuses and the young family receiving terrible news about their unborn child. What values did the two families hold dear, values to which they turned to help them make their decision?

The woman, impregnated with two fetuses, believed that she was entitled to say thank you, but I only want one child: like one chocolate or one pair of pants. Or, I want the boy, not the girl. The fetuses she was carrying had no intrinsic value to her. Her moral values were based on Utilitarianism; her quality-of-life, self-directed ethics of entitlement enabled her to see the fetus as a thing, an obstacle to her happiness, an inconvenience, a burden, like a hangnail, and so she turned to the medical profession and expected, as her unrestricted, absolute, human right, a selective abortion. There was no sense of guilt and shame in selecting one fetus to abort, because her entitlement ethic did not require that she choose between two opposing needs; her ethical values recognized only one person's needs—her own.

What of the young couple? They have been given terrible news: news that I can't imagine receiving. If they believe in the ethics of Utilitarianism, the decision is easy. The fetus will be a burden, taking away from their entitlement of happiness. If they view the fetus in an impersonal way, then abortion to them is not ending potential *human* life. It's more like simply removing a tumor. They know this fetus is imperfect, perhaps fatally so, and that it may suffer. What if they cannot bear the idea of their child suffering? In the ethics of entitlement, this young couple would have no problem with an abortion. There would be no moral dilemma, no conflict of rights or responsibilities. But what if they believe that each life is sacred?

Is there room in ethical monotheism for a woman to know in her heart that abortion is morally wrong, but also that for her it is the right choice? And this is the moral dilemma. A dilemma that arises only in an ethic that is based on rights and responsibilities and prioritizes the sanctity of life. An ethic that often forces us into making difficult decisions that take us into the ethical "gray zone."

In a perfect world, I think the vast majority of us would prefer to live without abortion. But this is not a perfect world. I doubt we can end abortion by proclamation. In the fourth century CE, John Chrysostom (which means "golden mouth") preached the importance of persuasion. One "cannot be dragged back by force, nor restrained by fear, but must be led by persuasion."[96]

Ethical monotheism makes it possible for us to have a discussion that balances the rights of the mother with the rights of the potential life. "Do not stand by while your neighbor's blood is shed" (Leviticus 19:16) is a commandment that speaks to a moral obligation, not a legal one. Our Western laws do not command me to save another person's life. Legally, I can stand by and watch one human being hurt another. Morally, that response would be reprehensible.

This commandment to not stand by while blood is shed can speak to both the potential mother and the potential human life.

Pregnancy, for all of our modern medicine, can endanger a woman's life. To demand that a woman continue to bear a child, to deny her the right to a legal abortion, could push her to a backroom butcher and the possibility of two deaths—hers and the fetus. As a society, we would be morally guilty of standing by while her blood is shed. Forcing a woman to carry to term can also conflict with the

---

commandment to "choose life; for you and your descendants" (Deuteronomy 30:19), if this pregnancy negatively affects her health to the point that her death is possible.

This commandment "Do not stand by while your neighbor's blood is shed," also speaks to the potential human life of a fetus. If one believes that a fetus is potential human life, whether life begins at conception or later, then approving abortion puts everyone involved in a position of standing by while blood—potential human life—is shed. This moral commandment also makes room for the rights of others to come to the table. It will make room for the rights of the father.

By law, a woman can enforce child support once paternity is proven. So a man, a potential father, has obligations to pay for a child he might not have known he had fathered. Yet if he learns that a woman has become pregnant with his child, he has no right to have that child. This moral law—"Do not stand by"—gives him rights. He has the right to prevent the shedding of blood by taking full responsibility for the child at birth. Yes, the woman must carry the fetus. But she, too, has moral responsibilities. She participated in the conception of this fetus. And then there are the rights of the grandparents-to-be: the fruit of the womb of the fruit of the womb. In a compassionate world, grandparents would have a place at the table regarding the continuation of a pregnancy.

> *We want to return to the Garden, before we were given free will and moral responsibility.*

These conflicting rights and responsibilities, based just on this one moral commandment, make abortion a moral dilemma that requires living in the grey zone between absolute right and absolute wrong. It is an uncomfortable place to be. We all prefer the calm of absolute knowledge of right and wrong. We want to return to the Garden before Adam and Eve ate of the fruit of knowledge of good and evil, before we were given free will with moral responsibility. But we can't. We have as our light the ethics we choose, and that choice directly affects the society we become.

Ethical monotheism ascribes to each individual a sacredness that is not afforded to us in the other ethical systems (except the Kantian). I believe it is better to start with an absolute definition of *human* than to start from a place where the definition of human is a moving target. The Judeo-Christian religio-ethic provides a space for us to make a very difficult decision without demeaning the meaning of *human*. Because this ethic comes with the knowledge that one can fall from grace and rise again, the Judeo-Christian ethic prevents us from denigrating the human being in an attempt to justify a difficult decision; because it certainly is easier to abort some *thing* rather than acknowledge the aborting of potential life. At the same time, when we attempt to take away the sanctity of life to make it easier to justify abortion, we take away the family's need for mourning the loss: because there is a loss.

This same ethic, an ethic that sanctifies all life, applies to our questions about the end of life. Do we as a society care for the weakest as we do the strongest? Do we accord the weakest members of our society the same rights and dignity that we do the strongest? Or do we think of the elderly through the lens of quality-of-life ethics and decide that they are as much a burden as would be an "imperfect" child, and so we help them out of this life?

Many decades ago, there was a television program, *The Twilight Zone*, hosted by Rod Serling. In one episode, "The Eye of the Beholder," we are brought into an operating room where we see the back of the heads of the staff bent over the surgical table. We hear the voice of a female patient begging the doctors to do whatever they can to fix her. We listen to the dialogue among the medical staff as they try to repair her body. We hear their sense of frustration. We watch as the nurses blot the sweat off the surgeon's brow.

Then the doctors sadly inform the patient that the procedure is a failure. She begs them to try again, but they tell her there is nothing more that can be done; she is defective. She knows she will now have to go to the special towns, the cities of refuge, set aside for defective people like her. We hear her crying and begging as the credits roll over the screen, and then we finally see the woman. She is gorgeous! In our day, she would be described as a supermodel, with her beautifully chiseled features, big, wide eyes, and long, wavy hair. And we wonder, what is so wrong with her that she needs to be hidden away? She appears to be the very definition of beautiful.

Then we see the faces of the surgeons and nurses as they remove their masks and commiserate about the poor woman. And we finally understand why they thought she needed "repairing." Because her face is indeed very different, shockingly different, from theirs. Their faces, which are all identical, are the epitome of perfection: . . . perfect pigs' faces.

XIII
GOD CREATED HEAVEN AND EARTH

Know this, children, that just as the house attests to the builder and the garment to the tailor and the door to the carpenter, the world is and will be God's testimonial; one has only to look at it to understand that what it affirms is God.

—Rabbi Akiva

Science and creation can live together side by side without being blasphemous one to the other. And at times they can intersect to provide wider depth and space for the soul to breathe, expand, break boundaries and feel limitless, at one with the universe and the Divine. I am in awe of the concepts of black holes, dark matter, and the big bang and the constant evolving, devolving, expanding and contracting that takes place in the universe and the natural world.

Each time science unearths something new about creation, another enigma presents itself. It is like opening successive Russian nesting dolls. We can choose to imbue the science, the cold hard facts of creation through evolution, with sacredness because we are discussing the most sacred thing in existence: life. We can choose to believe that human life has intrinsic value because we choose to believe that we are created in God's image and that each of us is filled with His divine spark. I have no logical reason to believe this, no indisputable proof: I have what Baruch Spinoza called "an intellectual love of God," which makes room for the possibility for me to believe that a transcendent, unknowable Power lies just behind the primordial big bang.

To deny the scientific facts of evolution, carbon dating, and fossils is to deny the existence of half of our brain and the whole of our soul. If God did not want us to discover the origin of our being, God would not have placed all the clues before us. Instead,

He would have placed stumbling blocks before us, to trip us up, to blind us from the truth He placed before us. There are those who say that the devil turns people away from creationism. Yet if that were true, then we would give to the devil greater power than the power we give to God.

Sir Charles Darwin, the author of *On the Origin of Species* and the theory of evolution, was a man of faith who studied multiple disciplines, including theology, geology, geography, culture, and fossils. He saw the natural world much the same way as his contemporary, Charles Lyell, saw the earth: as constantly changing in small and gradual increments. We are part of nature, so we too must be in flux, adapting, changing, and evolving.

Darwin's theories of evolution did not take away from his sense of awe at the origin of species. He referred to it as the "mystery of mysteries."[97] We can continue, today, to bring Darwin and God to the same table. I know the place of evolution in scientific knowledge. My left brain, the analytical side, understands it completely. It's the right brain, the one that experiences all boundaries slipping away, that lets me imagine the hand of God, the ultimate artist working behind the scenes. There is no need for shame or a sense of guilt, nor to explain or justify the presence of something ethereal at play in evolution. Our brain gives us the joy of perceiving reality in a way that makes sense to each of us uniquely. We choose the metaphors that best help us comprehend our world. As we become more knowledgeable about our world, our view of God changes. We come to realize that evolution is part of God's plan from creation.

At Snolab, near Sudbury, Ontario, Canada, scientists like Dr. Fraser Duncan, Snolab's assistant director, are searching for dark matter, which "causes large-scale structure and evolution of the universe. Normal matter would not have been able to coalesce into stars and planets if dark matter hadn't been there to guide the process." Physicists know that dark matter exists, but so far it has proven stubbornly challenging to spot in real life. As Dr. Duncan said, "You're looking for something that we don't know is there.

[97] Janet Browne, *Darwin's Origin of Species*, 28.

We don't know for a fact that dark matter exists, but there's very good circumstantial evidence for it."[98]

One must never confuse religion with science or use the Bible as a source of scientific fact. The Bible is not, and never was, a science textbook. The language that Dr. Duncan uses to describe the search for dark matter, though, is like describing a religious pilgrimage. Scientists are searching for the Holy Grail of the beginning of the universe. This search is filled with religious metaphors and similes. Some commentators refer to the Higgs boson, the particle that is responsible for creating mass, as the "God particle." I think it is that way because science, like religion, is involved in the *mysterium* and *tremendum* of creation.

In religious terms, the *mysterium* and *tremendum*, "fear and trembling," refer to our relationship with God. We are pulled in closer and closer, wanting to know more and more about Him, yet as we get closer, there is a sense of trepidation, a fear of getting too close. We stand back in awe. If we get too close, too fast, we may get burned by a living fire. So at the last minute we pull back, take a breather, and then, unable to resist, we start the journey again. In science, the mystery of the beginning of the universe calls us; there is an urge to uncover its secrets. Scientists push forward, perhaps with moments of trepidation, hoping for answers, yet fearing the answer will elude them. The idea that Dr. Duncan knows, perhaps in his soul, that dark matter exists, gives his search purpose, meaning, and value just as my search for God gives me purpose, meaning, and value. Science is searching for the beginning of life, to which religion adds the sacred.

God is continually involved in creation and evolution. His word continues to spread through the universe side by side with the energy that burst forth with the initial Big Bang. We are expected to continue to evolve and develop better moral discernment based on the teachings of this monotheistic God. We are compelled to question, question, question, if we are to be honest children of God.

---

[98] Diane Weber Bederman, "My Search for God Gives Me Purpose," The Huffington Post, http:// www.huffingtonpost.ca/ diane-bederman/ religion- god_ b_ 3786080.html.

Questioning is part of our nature, just as Abraham and Moses questioned God. If we stop questioning, it means we have stopped noticing; we have lost awareness; we are losing our sense of awe and wonder—and our souls will shrivel and die. The German philosopher Martin Heidegger wrote that "questions are piety, the prayer of human thought."[99] It isn't always the answer that is so important. Discovery and innovation and contemplation require very good questions.

---

[99] Steiner, *Nostalgia*, 59.

XIV
WHO IS THIS GOD WHO MAKES DEMANDS OF US, WHO CARES FOR US?

God was in this place & I, I did not know.
—Lawrence Kushner

Moses was a shepherd in the land of Midian. He was a quiet man who walked the land, caring for his flock. Who knows how many times he had walked the same paths, across the same streams? Who knows how many times he had walked past that small, rather innocuous bush at the edge of the path? It was a burning bush; rather hard to miss. Then one day he saw. And he knew. On that day, he was ready to be aware (see Exodus 3:2–4).

God is always waiting at the edges of the path, patiently waiting for us to be aware, to look, to see, to know. God is infinite in His patience and His trust in us to listen, to learn, to grow more conscious of our responsibilities to care and show compassion for others. As time has passed from the moment of creation, His Word has spread, broader and wider, filled with greater levels of meaning, waiting for us to see and know that all of us who follow His teachings are of the same family. And like members of any family, some of us travel different paths to arrive at the same location. God is waiting there, patiently, at the edges, for us to become aware of His desire for us to hold each other up, not tear each other down or demean or diminish the paths taken by the members of His family. He is waiting, in the fire, in the burning bush that is never consumed, waiting for us to be aware of our need to love and respect others.

How do I call God? What do I call Him? To name someone is to limit them, to place boundaries, to define, to separate, to make smaller, more manageable, perhaps to diminish. To give to God a particular name, to attempt to translate the unknowable, unpronounceable Tetragrammaton (the Hebrew four-letter acronym for God's name) is to limit our wonderings of Him, to put our miniscule boundaries around the *mysterium* and *tremendum* of the Divine. To name God as we name a person is to make God a mere mortal.

What is in a name? Freud wrote, "A name . . . is only a label to distinguish a thing from other similar things, not a syllabus, a description of its content or definition."[100] There are 91 words in Hebrew for the English translation God; Jehovah; Yahweh. God is a constellation of meanings. Moses wanted to know the name of the God of Abraham, Isaac, and Jacob. Who is this God? The answer: "I was I am I will be." There is no name. There is a presence of an absence.

For us mortals, this is a conundrum. We communicate via symbols. How can we understand something with no name? Imagine a tree. If ten people are in a room and are asked to describe what they think of when they hear the word or see the letters for *tree*. You will have many answers. Some will see an evergreen. Others will see a magnificent red maple in the fall. Some will see birds' nests in the tree. Others will describe the starkness of trees in winter. Naming defines, limits, closes, reduces, and gives boundaries to things: This is how it looks. This is how long it will live. These are the properties of this thing that I named with a symbol.

To name God is to limit God; it is to put boundaries around this energy; this ethereal, ephemeral being. We have limits; mortality. God is limitless. It is that sense of limitlessness that brings past, present, and future together, connecting all that was, that is, and will be. This forces us to think about those who came before us and those who will come after, so that we care for what is. This is the religious meaning of *grounding*. We are grounded by and in our history and by our rituals, symbols, traditions and beliefs, and our common shared stories. This is Spirituality—past, present, future; I was, I am, I will be. I am the place. I am the rock. I am just and merciful. I am compassionate, full of loving kindness.

---

[100] Carveth, *The Analyst's Metaphors*, 491-560.

The divine spark within each of us connects us to the limitlessness of God and the universe. And when we think of this connection, when we allow ourselves to be truly aware and conscious of that connection, we will care for others, we will care for the stranger, we will cry for the other; we will develop greater empathy for all. One soul connected to another to God. This unknowable God, who commands and demands of us, becomes known to us through our own imaginings, through our own unique spiritual needs, through a self-reflecting respect between one and the greater cosmos.

To live with the concept of a God without a name is challenging, for we are genetically predisposed to label and categorize. How does one live with One who has no borders? How does one begin to describe One without limits? Without a name, are you an enemy or are you a friend? How does one live with so much uncertainty? How do we communicate about God if He has no name that is common to all of us, that immediately brings to mind a concept, a referent to that about which we are speaking? It forces us to live with tension. It forces us to be tolerant and accepting of the referents that each of has for the concept God, just as we accept the referent for the concept of tree that each of us describes.

> There was a great and mighty wind, splitting the mountains and shattering rocks by the power of God; but God was not in the wind. After the wind—an earthquake; but God was not in the earthquake. And after the earthquake—fire; but God was not in the fire; And after the fire—the sound of delicate silence. 1 Kings 19:11b–12

These are the words of God speaking to his prophet, Elijah. Unlike His revelation at Mount Sinai, where He made Himself known to the people through the rumble of thunder and streaks of lightning and in dense cloud, or to Moses where He waited patiently for Moses to be aware of Him in the fire, here God called softly to Elijah in a still small voice, beckoning him to come and listen. The time of God bellowing out to us is long past. He speaks to us from within; from that still small voice. It is the voice of our moral response to His ethical teachings.

I was once sharing stories with another grandmother. She told me about her granddaughter, Maggie. Maggie was a beautiful, healthy baby, but at two she was diagnosed with a brain tumor, which led to blindness. When Maggie was five, she read and wrote in Braille. She loved to write letters to people—every single day. She took after her father in this respect. Her grandmother had taught Maggie's father to write a letter to God when feeling conflicted or confused and leave it overnight, sleep on it, open himself to the still small voice within, and then reread the letter in the morning to see if he could work out his problem. One day Maggie wrote a letter to the poor. She asked her mother to mail her Barbie doll with the letter. At only five years of age, Maggie was blessed with great compassion, almost as if she had an old soul living within her. Maggie teaches us that we do not need eyes to see. We can see from the inside out, not just the outside in. Sight comes from the still small voice within, *the voice of wisdom.*

> *I move in every creature . . . in everyone, and I delve into them all . . . and I am a voice speaking softly . . . I dwell in the silence . . . I am the real voice, I cry out in everyone and they recognize me, since a seed indwells them.*[101]

Those of us who believe in God must look at every human being as souls who are spiritually connected, for if we believe in God, then we believe that we are children of God and that we are all members of one family. We are all part of the same initial burst of energy that began with a bang when in the beginning, "Was, Is, and Will Be" created.

---

[101] Pagels, *Revelations*, 99.

XV
I WILL MAKE FOR YOU A SIGN

*So act that your principle of action might
safely be made a law for the whole world.*

— Immanuel Kant

Nineteenth-century philosopher John Stuart Mill wrote that, through logical deduction, we can see tendencies in human social development. We can evaluate the development of a society by studying history. We can then discover the laws of social progress and development and predict the probability that certain social results can be expected. For Mill, social well-being was necessary for individual well-being.[102] History has proven that cultures rise and fall and that not all cultures are equally good or acceptable. Science teaches us that the culture in which we live may affect our moral discernment, because our behaviors are (to some extent) the result of a mixing of genes and culture. In a sense, we have a genetic memory that is passed down through our culture's *memes*, or units of deep cultural information. I referred to memes in chapter eight, A Light Unto the Nations, when talking about the citizens of Le Chambon-sur-lignon. Both genes and memes are subject to the theory of the survival of the fittest: "Members of a species with genes or memes best adapted to survival will prevail over those least adapted."[103]

Western culture has a history of thousands of years. It began with Abraham 3500 years ago. Peoples and nations have come and gone, but the ethical concepts described in the Bible remain strong today because they are the fittest of all memes from the past to the present. The time has come to defend Western culture and civilization against the attacks made by both the Left and the Right, because they tear away at the very essence, the very core, of our

---

[102] S. E. Frost, *Basic Teachings of the Great Philosophers*, 202.
[103] Somerville, *Imagination*, 99.

society, our culture, our sense of community, our priorities, our values and ethical systems; values that have proven over time to be open, forward thinking, and inquisitive. "Don't let Western civilization—the best and most humane form of civilization developed by mankind—perish by default."[104]

Some cultures preach going with the flow, repressing one's desire, losing one's sense of self. Other cultures are steeped in victimhood, defeatism, and a flight from responsibility. There are hierarchical cultures that declare some people as having less value than others. This can lead to a defeatist attitude among the "less worthy," as their ability to dream is crushed from birth. In India, within the Hindu caste system, there is a group of people known as the Mushahar (Dalits), also known as the "Untouchables." Solely by virtue of their birth they are considered to be too impure to eat, walk, or bathe among their neighbors. The girls are the lowest form of Dalit: they only get to eat the last scraps of food at the edge of the pot. Some people hide behind the idea of "God's will," much like others hide behind the secular expression *que sera sera*: "whatever will be, will be."

These ideas predate ethical monotheism, going back to when it was believed that the gods decided one's fate, but they breed defeatism, a sense of helplessness, victimization, and entitlement. Individuals in such a culture believe they have been born into a space and a place from which there is no escape, into a society that is innately unfair and where they have no real free will. Thus the individual has no incentive, no compulsion, to find answers or to change their circumstances. They just continue to wait, like someone waiting for Godot. Leaving everything in God's hands can also prevent us from showing compassion and empathy, because we can blame someone's problem on Him and so excuse ourselves from helping them.

Despite all these valid criticisms of other cultures, the famous anthropologist Franz Boas wrote as recently as the mid-twentieth

---

[104] George Jonas, "The Ten Commandments of Sending Your Troops to War," Full Comment, *National Post*, April 2, 2011, http://fullcomment.nationalpost.com/2011/04/02/george-jonas-the-10-commandments-of-sending-your-troops-to-war/.

century that there are no inferior or superior cultures, but that all cultures are equal.[105] This is nothing more than cultural relativism. And history has proven Boas completely wrong. After seeing the unspeakable savagery perpetrated by the Nazis, the Marxists, and the Islamist fundamentalists, no decent person is obligated to consider all cultures, all ideas, or all cultural practices as equals. We do not have to bow down before their idols, even when they are presented in the latest fashion of ideological clothing and by our own intellectuals.

> *After seeing the unspeakable savagery perpetrated by the Nazis, the Marxists, and the Islamist fundamentalists, no decent person is obligated to consider all cultures, all ideas, or all cultural practices as equals.*

For example, the highly esteemed English philosopher Bertrand Russell (1872–1970) believed that the survival of democracy required absolute tolerance and understanding of others.[106] Russell was a brilliant thinker and he is touted as someone society should respect, but his view of tolerance has led to the rise in extremist multiculturalism and the propaganda campaign of political correctness that our governments, schools, intellectual elite, and much of the media are promoting.

Obviously, democracy does require acceptance of different beliefs and customs. That is a fundamental requirement of democracy. But we should not feel compelled to tolerate and accept any and all aspects of any and all cultures. Such extreme tolerance would be incredibly foolish and naive. It would not only be like allowing a complete stranger to move into your home where he feels so comfortable that he moves the furniture around; it would be to hand him full ownership rights. One of the many wonders of our Western societies is that we can and do accept and integrate immigrants from all ethnic and cultural backgrounds: but we don't,

---

[105] Franz Boas, *The Limitations of the Comparative Method of Anthropology*, 270-280.
[106] Andrew David Irvine, "Bertrand Russell," *Stanford Encyclopedia of Philosophy*, December 1995 (revised March 2013), http://plato.stanford.edu/entries/russell/.

nor should we, accept all their cultural practices. We are a multi-ethnic society, tolerant of all ethnicities; we are not—nor is any culture in the world—a truly multicultural society: fully tolerant of all other cultures. That sort of absolute tolerance—multiculturalism—is cultural suicide dressed in Versace.

The seeds of destruction of Western civilization lie in an irrational view of its basic principles of freedom. Political freedom does not give anyone the right to demand customs or rituals that weaken the very foundations of democracy. It was Jean-Jacques Rousseau who in 1762 wrote in *Of The Social Contract, Or Principles of Political Right* that one of the building blocks of a healthy society is the agreement with which a person enters into civil society. "The contract essentially binds people into a community that exists for mutual preservation. In entering into civil society, people sacrifice the physical freedom of being able to do whatever they please, but they gain the civil freedom of being able to think and act rationally and morally."[107] Citizens enter a democratic community voluntarily. By doing so, they are choosing to accept what has been established as the best interests of that society: the common good, and the general will, which expresses what is best for that state as a whole. This requires a delicate social balancing act of both rights and responsibilities that is at its best in a democracy. Democracy is not a suicide pact.

Democracy is not a suicide pact.

The word "tolerance" has about it a sense of begrudgingly accepting something not to our liking. If I am expected to tolerate your ways in order for you to feel welcome, then surely you also have some responsibilities to me, your host. Acceptance and inclusiveness should not include the right to destroy the accepting culture from within. In September 2104, David Cameron, Prime Minister of Great Britain, stated this: "We are an open, tolerant and free nation. But we cannot stand by and allow our openness to be confused with a tolerance of extremism. Adhering to British values is not an option or a choice—it is a duty for those who live in these

---

[107] Jean-Jacques Rousseau, "Of The Social Contract, Or Principles of Political Right," http://www.sparknotes.com/philosophy/socialcontract/characters.html/.

islands. It is only by standing up for these values that we will defeat extremism, protect our way of life and keep all our people safe."[108]

It is not incumbent upon any culture, in the name of tolerance, to accept every value of another culture. Rather, it is incumbent on "the other"—those who have freely chosen to come to the West— to be tolerant of and open to all of our Western cultural possibilities. And it is up to us the host to assist in every way possible, to help newcomers let go of the ties that enslave them to their past, in order that they can embrace the freedom that the West embodies.

Keep in mind, there are cultures that do not believe that women have any inherent value; these cultures cover up their women and often do not educate their girls. There are cultures that live with child labor, child brides, child soldiers, stoning of women, and honor-based violence, including honor killings. There are patriarchal cultures that promote the aborting of female fetuses and female infanticide[109] and that sell their children. There is only one moral position that we in the West can take toward these beliefs: we must condemn them. And when we do, we are making a statement that we are against moral and cultural relativism, that multiculturalism and extreme tolerance are wrong.

Now, what happens when people from theocratic and autocratic countries come to the West with their repressive culture? Do we tolerate the behaviors that come with them? Ayaan Hirsi Ali, in her book *The Nomad*, writes about Muslim schools in the United States today "where girls learn all day long to be subservient and to lower their eyes, to veil themselves to symbolize suppression of their individual will. They are taught to internalize male superiority."[110] To veil or not veil is one of the cultural differences that has led to a period of cultural conflict within the West.

I had the opportunity to travel to Egypt prior to the Arab Spring. What an extraordinary country: the history, the architecture,

---

[108] "Former top lawyer says anti-terror laws 'may not be legal'," ITV News, September 1, 2014, http://www.itv.com/news/update/2014-09-01/pm-adhering-to-british-values-not-a-choice/.
[109] Adam Jones, "Case Study: Female Infanticide," Gendercide.org, http://www.gendercide.org/case_infanticide.html.
[110] Hirsi Ali, *The Nomad*, 129.

the food, and the people! A young Muslim woman was our guide one steamy hot day. Because it was so hot, I dressed lightly but modestly, in light-colored, loose cotton pants and shirt. This lovely woman, perhaps in her early twenties, was wearing blue jeans with a long black skirt over the top. She was wearing a dark, long-sleeved, polyester tee shirt and over top of it a short-sleeved white tee shirt. She also wore a headscarf and a big hat and when we were out in the sun, she put on gloves. Needless to say, her layers of clothing were more suited to summer in the Arctic than to the Sahara Desert.

We were having lunch by the Nile when we talked about veils. She explained to me that Egyptian women consider it high praise when a husband wants his wife to wear a veil when she goes out. It is his way of saying that his wife is very beautiful and he does not want to share her beauty with other men. It is a lovely compliment that enables a woman, wanting to be seen as beautiful, to choose to hide herself from society.

That is a noble and possibly desirable sentiment. Not dressing immodestly in public is certainly a commendable and courteous habit, both for men and women.

But to claim that the veil is used only for modesty's sake is dishonest. It is also a symbol of suppression and oppression and is a statement that women are "less than." The veil, just like the even more extreme *burka* (the full-body veil required for women in Saudi Arabia, Yemen, and some other Muslim cultures), is used to keep women separate from and unequal to the rest of society. And this practice is intrinsically objectionable in a democracy.

Rousseau's social contract, by its very nature, requires trust. Here in the West, much of that trust has developed because we recognize, we are able to "see," one another. Police officers, judges, members of government, and all those in public service always have their faces uncovered. A democratic society requires this public openness to foster and preserve the trust required for democracy to function.

So having many citizens wearing a veil does not meet the standard for the social contract in a democratic society, because veiling your face denies me the very basic right to see you. And that right to see you must trump a "religious" belief that a woman must or should cover her face. Whether a woman is forced to don the veil or chooses to (although how would we ever know for certain that the woman was *not* coerced by her family?), there can be no justification in a democratic society for always covering one's face in public.

If large numbers of women in our Western democracies are choosing to wear a veil, then it speaks to the failure of our culture to inculcate in our citizens this great legacy of freedom.

As the former Archbishop of Canterbury, Lord Carey of Clifton, said: "By embracing multiculturalism and the idea that every culture and belief is of equal value we have betrayed our own traditions."[111]

Former Spanish Prime Minister José María Aznar wrote in 2010: "The West is going through a period of confusion over the shape of the world's future. To a great extent, this confusion is caused by a kind of masochistic self-doubt over our own identity; by the rule of political correctness; by a multiculturalism that forces us to our knees before others."[112]

Our culture is one of great openness and equality, and this openness and tolerance is a great gift to the world. But we must not give a higher priority to tolerance (also called "diversity" or "inclusiveness") than to protecting our own moral values. We should not allow the cultural gap between us and newcomers to our countries to be filled with moral and cultural relativism and with intolerant behaviors that we condemn in other countries.

Thousands of years ago, the Bible, the Judeo-Christian culture, questioned the sacrifice of women on the altar of family honor. There is a story in the Bible about Dinah, Jacob's daughter. "Shechem, son of Hamor the Hivite, headman of the region, saw her (Dinah), seized her and forced her to sleep with him" (Genesis

---

[111] Matthew Holehouse, "Multiculturalism has brought us honour killings and Sharia law," *London Telegraph*, August 24, 2014, http:// www.telegraph.co.uk/ news/worldnews/ middleeast/ syria/ 11053646/ Multiculturalism-has-brought-us-honour-killings-and-Sharia-law-says-Archbishop.html.

[112] Jose Maria Aznar, "If Israel Goes Down, We All Go Down," *The London Times*, June 17, 2010, http:// www.worldjewishcongress.org/ en/ main/ showNews/ id/ 9401.

33:2). Shechem then wanted to marry Dinah. That was not to be. "Shechem had insulted Israel by sleeping with Jacob's daughter—a thing totally unacceptable" (Genesis 33:8). Jacob's sons, Simeon and Levi, "each took his sword and advanced unopposed against the town and slaughtered all the males. They killed Hamor and his son Shechem with the sword, removed Dinah from Shechem's house and came away" (Genesis 33:25–27). Jacob responded, "You have done me an ill turn by bringing me into bad odor with the people of the region, the Canaanites and the Perrizites. I have few men, whereas they will unite against me and destroy me and my family. They retorted: "Should our sister be treated like a whore?" (Genesis 33:30–31).

We never hear from Dinah about her wishes or feelings. Was she raped, treated like a whore, or did she care for Shechem? Did she want to marry him? After all, he was from a different tribe; a different culture. But apparently no one asked her. Her brothers did not consider her wishes. She was not considered an equal. Her brothers decided that she would not be allowed to marry outside her tribe and her culture, since they felt that would bring dishonor on their family. But Jacob was not pleased with the brothers' behavior. He knew it could lead to tribal warfare.

> *Simeon and Levi are brothers—*
> *in carrying out their malicious plans.*
> *May my soul not enter their council*
> *nor my heart join their company,*
> *for in their rage they have killed men*
> *and hamstrung oxen at their whim.*
> *Accursed be their rage for its ruthlessness,*
> *their wrath for its ferocity. I shall disperse them in Jacob,*
> *I shall scatter them through Israel.*

Genesis 49:5–7

Western culture has continued to develop as an open system, inviting the economically, socially, and politically disadvantaged from other cultures to live in our free society. Each group of immigrants has brought its culture, its religious beliefs, clothing, food, and language. And over time, their children and their children's children have acculturated to the moral value system of Western culture that honors personal freedom and free will. At the same time, each group has retained aspects of its religion in the privacy of their own homes. All immigrants, at one time or another, must balance the ties that bind them to the culture they have left with the bonds that must be broken in order to "Go forth" into the new home they have chosen for themselves and their children.

XVI
NOSTALGIA FOR THE ABSOLUTE

*Life is likened unto two roads: one of fire and
one of ice. If you walk in the one, you will be
burned, and if in the other, you will be frozen.
What shall one do? Walk in the middle.*
— Abraham Joshua Heschel, *The Sabbath*

Those of us who have been blessed with the miracle of being
born into Western civilization have been raised in a culture that
promotes freedom and free will. We exercise our free will on a daily
basis, often without giving it second thought. Going to the grocery
store is an exercise in free will. Think of the last time you stood in
the cereal aisle: you are presented with more than fifty choices in
cereals! You look at the boxes of hot cereal, fast-cooking oats,
slow-cooking organic. Next you come face to face with the cold
cereals, for children or the whole family or just for adults: cereals
that cater to heart and colon health. Maybe spelt would be better
than oats? As you shift your weight from one foot to another, you
examine the fine print on this box and then that one, comparing
them. How much sodium? How many calories? Is there any protein
or fiber, sugar, artificial flavor, or ingredients that you cannot
pronounce? Finally, there is the price check.

But when was the last time you sat down with your family and
discussed the best moral and ethical system for your family, your
community, or your nation? This is food for the soul. Atheists,
agnostics, and humanists demean ethical monotheism, but I haven't
heard a cogent alternative. There is a lot of feeling-based opinion
that tends to be 100% fact-free, but I rarely hear opinion based on
critical thinking and knowledge. Western society has been exposed
to many cultures, philosophies, and religions that fear change and
hold tenaciously to the past, not realizing that the time is fleeting
and the past is long gone and not meant to be retrieved. Fear is the
enemy of ethical monotheism. Secular and religious fundamentalists

know this and take advantage of our deep-seated nostalgia for the absolute.[113] They lure us with their own certitudes down a path to fundamentalism.

Fundamentalism—whether secular or religious—tempts us to go back to the Garden of Eden, where we do not think, or choose, or grow, or transform. Fundamentalism thrives where fear hides and survives. Machiavelli wrote, "Men do you harm either because they fear you or hate you."[114] Throughout history, fundamentalism has led to war, carnage, and genocide because of the divisiveness in its ideology, a black and white, Manichean duality of thinking. Fundamentalism is closed to any synthesis of ideas because it requires fear as its foundation in order to successfully spread its propaganda, be it religious or secular. Secular fundamentalists frighten me as much religious ones who extol the virtue of obeying an autocratic, despotic, unrelenting, dogmatic, wish-fulfilling deity. As Barack Obama, in his "Call to Renewal" keynote address on June 28, 2006, in Washington D.C., said:

> Secularists are wrong when they ask believers to leave their religion at the door before entering into the public square. Frederick Douglas, Abraham Lincoln, William Jennings Bryan, Dorothy Day, Martin Luther King—indeed, the majority of great reformers in American history—were not only motivated by faith, but repeatedly used religion to argue for their cause. So to say that men and women should not inject their "personal morality" into public policy debates is a practical absurdity. Our law is by definition a codification of morality, much of it grounded in the Judeo-Christian tradition.[115]

Pope Benedict, speaking in Britain in September of 2010, said, "Religion . . . is not a problem for legislators to solve, but a vital contributor to the national conversation."[116]

---

[113] Steiner, Nostalgia, 5.
[114] Paul Strathern, The Artist, The Philosopher, and The Warrior, 405.
[115] Sandel, Justice, 246.
[116] Pope Benedict XVI, Address to Parliament, Westminster Hall, London, September 17, 2010, http:// www.vatican.va/ holy_father/ benedict_xvi/ speeches/ 2010/ september/ documents/ hf_ben-xvi_spe_20100917_societa-civile_en.html.

Ethical monotheism is not the enemy.

Belief in the ethical God of the Christians and Jews counterbalances egoism and the idolization of another human being. I cannot place belief in any man perfecting himself. The evidence is overwhelmingly to the contrary. I wrote about that earlier, in my chapter "The Snake Tempted Me," about the Enlightenment and the rise of secularism. More people have died from wars that embraced secular fundamentalist propaganda than have been killed in wars based on religious differences. *Encyclopedia of Wars* authors Charles Phillips and Alan Axelrod document the history of recorded warfare. From their list of 1,763 wars, only 123 are classified as involving a religious cause; these wars account for **less than 7 percent** of all wars and **less than 2 percent** of all people killed in warfare. It is estimated that more than 160 million civilians were killed in genocides in the twentieth century alone, with nearly 100 million killed by the Communist states of USSR and China. Think of Joseph Stalin, Mao Zedong, Pol Pot, Idi Amin, Kim Jong-il, and Adolph Hitler.

Why do we allow ourselves to give up our free will and instead be swayed by others? Why do we so easily forget God's admonition, "Beware of letting your heart be seduced; if you go astray, serve other gods and bow down to them . . . you will quickly perish"? (Deuteronomy 11:16–17). In his novel *The Brothers Karamazov* (1880), the Russian author, Dostoyevsky, writes about the burden of freedom in his parable "The Grand Inquisitor." In the story, Jesus comes to Seville, Spain, in the late-fifteenth century, at the time of the Spanish Inquisition. He is taken prisoner by the Grand Inquisitor and questioned.

> *The Grand Inquisitor tells Jesus that humanity is too weak to bear the gift of freedom. It does not seek freedom but bread—not the divine bread promised by Jesus, but ordinary earthly bread. People will worship whoever gives them bread, for they need their rulers to be gods. The Grand Inquisitor tells Jesus that his teaching has been amended to deal with humanity as it really is: "We have corrected Thy work and have founded it on miracle, mystery and authority. And men rejoiced that they were again led like sheep, and that the*

terrible gift that brought them such suffering was, at last, lifted from their hearts."[117]

Fundamentalism thrives on this need for authority, a type of idol worship that encourages submission rather than freedom. Leaders who control the word also control power. The power and the word held together in one hand can be dangerous, whether the word is the word of a secular tyrant or the word of God. Pervez Hoodbhoy, one of South Asia's leading nuclear physicists, wrote, "Whenever and wherever religious fundamentalism dominates, blind faith clouds objective and rational thinking. If such forces take hold in a society, they create a mindset unfavorable for critical inquiry, with its need to question wisdom."[118] The same can be said of secular fundamentalism.

And that is why we must remember the commandment:

> *I am the Lord your God who brought you out of Egypt, where you lived as slaves. You shall have no other gods to rival Me. You shall not make yourself a carved image or any likeness or anything in heaven above or earth beneath or in the waters under the earth. You shall not bow down to them or serve them. For I, Yahweh, your God, am a jealous God.* Exodus 20:1–5

I have no doubt that religion can be a crutch in times of peril. Many of us turn and return to God when we are frightened. I have. But the religion of the Bible was never meant to simplify and replace thought. Religion practiced that way removes all ambiguity and doubt and so all need for faith. Everything is made to be black or white with no shades of gray. Faith becomes fixed. Feeling replaces thought, and one is taught to trust the heart, not the head. It is far easier to persuade the heart with oratory than it is to persuade the head with fact.

Fundamentalism chisels away at free will by teaching its followers not to question. When one is taught exactly what to think and precisely how not to believe, curiosity and inquisitiveness are lost. Instead of seeing our human mission as discovering God

---

[117] John Gray, *Straw Dogs,* 122.
[118] Tarek Fatah, *The Jew is Not My Enemy,* 183.

through reason and to evoke the powers of reason, fundamentalists focus their flock on personal salvation, having them give their will over to their preachers and the "will of God." But if we are completely under the control of God's will, there is no room for our free will.

The Bible teaches us that we are to be students and seekers of knowledge all our lives, and to consult our conscience through the study of Scripture. "Learn and interpret, search and examine, and act according to the conclusions that appear to you to be fully attested by solid evidence."[119] When Adam and Eve were removed from the Garden of Eden, God withdrew his total control and authority over them, forcing them to think for themselves, and to develop the free will that had led to their expulsion. Bahya Ben Joseph wrote in the twelfth century that searching for truth opens a man's soul to the flow of divine grace.[120] We are all Adam and Eve.

When the primary purpose of religion is seen merely as personal salvation based on a narrowly defined will of God (predetermination), the needs of the entire community can be displaced, because the focus is on the personal and not the universal. So if someone fails to achieve a mansion, let alone a room in the mansion, this failure can be blamed solely on them, without looking at the broader picture of failures within the social fabric of the community. But Paul wrote that we rely on God, who has called us to be partners—co-creators—in community, united in actions and concerns. The religion of the Bible is not meant to be used as an instrument to bludgeon followers into submission or pit one against the other. With the focus squarely on the individual, though, social justice for all is the loser. And God weeps.

True believers in the God of the Bible know the importance of caring for others, for the community. Jesus said, "Do unto others as you would have them do into you." This is the Golden Rule. Jesus, a rabbi who preached in the Galilee, was well versed in expressing the essence of the moral life.[121] He was well aware of the admonition in Leviticus 19:18: "Thou shalt love thy neighbor as

[119] Agus, *Thought*, 149.
[120] Ibid., 174.
[121] Joseph Hertz, *Ethics of the Fathers*, 44–5.

thyself." Tobit, who lived in the eighth century BCE and whose works are part of the Catholic and Orthodox canon, decreed, "What is displeasing to thyself, that do not unto any other."

Jesus would have been familiar with the writings of the second-century BCE Rabbi Ben Sira, whose wisdom writings are now part of the Catholic canon, and who said, "Honor thy neighbor as thyself." In the second half of the first century CE, after the destruction of the Second Temple, Rabbi Akiva declared, "Thou shalt love thy neighbor as thyself." And then Ben Azzai followed with the teaching that "all men are created in the Divine image, and, therefore, all are our fellowmen are entitled to human love." Jesus preached the Golden Rule to His apostles and his followers, who passed it down through the generations to Jesus's followers today.

Some people find it necessary to question the intentions of God, and they wonder, "Did I bring this tragedy on myself? Did I not honor God appropriately?" God created all living things and then created humans in His image. But humankind disappointed God and He regretted His creation. And so the Flood began. It was after the Flood that God repented: "Never again will I curse the earth because of human beings, because their heart contrives evil from infancy. Never again will I strike down every living thing as I have done" (Genesis 8:21). God made a sign to demonstrate this covenant: the rainbow. And each time a rainbow appears in the sky, God "will recall the covenant between Myself and you and every living creature" (Genesis 9:15).

Abraham argued with God to save Sodom and Gomorrah for the sake of only ten righteous people after God threatened to wipe out the entire group of people. After the Israelites built the golden calf in the desert, God was prepared to wipe out the people again, but Moses argued with Him and God relented. It is not rational that this forgiving, infinitely patient, all-loving God would inflict pain on an individual because of a lapse of judgement or behavior. To believe such a thing is to bring upon oneself untold pain, misery, and unredemptive suffering.

Having the certainty of a loving, eternal Creator at the center of the universe and of our existence leaves no room for a human tyrant—whether secular or religious—to rule over us with a rod of fear. Having God in the center of our lives keeps us balanced between extremes, because He is the God of compassion, justice, and mercy. If we hold these attributes dear and close to us, we will remember to honor God and to follow His commandments—and then we will not fear freedom. We will instead be justifiably wary of those who try to put themselves in the center of our life and tell us to follow them.

"The central problem in the Bible is not God, but man. The Bible is a book about man, rather than man's book about God."[122] The Author of the Bible is open and without limits. Our experience of Him ought to be the same. By reading the Bible only literally, we lose all the rich and thick layers of metaphor, layers of meaning that can be peeled away by each reader who then interprets the author through his or her unique lens. Fundamentalists, who prefer a literal or manifest interpretation of the Bible, disenfranchise the true believer from his ethical God as they prevent the word from constantly evolving and continually creating. We were never meant to read the Bible solely as an objective text: a book with only one possible meaning, some kind of "Immaculate Perception." The Bible does not say to limit ourselves to the manifest meanings of its words. Rather, it invites us to its limitlessness, to the limitlessness of the human journey. It is not a book written in stone. It was written on stone, to last forever.

Literary criticism teaches that, as readers, we must discover the meaning of the piece by uncovering the author's motives and intentions. Authority is in the hand of the author, and there is no room for the reader's interpretation. I remember, in my late teens, questioning my English professor about the meaning of Joseph Conrad's *Heart of Darkness*. My job as a student, my teacher said, was to discover what the author meant; what he wanted me to know. But I could not understand how I was supposed to divine what the author had been thinking or what he had wanted me to learn. After all, I wasn't a psychic. And I could not understand why it was so important to know what the author was thinking when he wrote certain passages. I had no understanding of the metaphors he was using. I didn't know that a river was more than a river or that

---

[122] Abraham Joshua Heschel, *Moral Grandeur and Spiritual Audacity*, 408.

Africa was more than a continent and the location of the novel. I was so frustrated in my inability to understand what the professor wanted, that I gave up trying to find any personal meaning in the novel. How sad. There is so much meaning to Conrad's story, but I was so frustrated in class that to this day I have not reread it. What a loss.

When literary criticism later began to focus on the reader's right to find their own pathway into the story, the author no longer had a monopoly on meaning. The reader was encouraged to find entrance points into the story that spoke uniquely to her. We find our way into literature through the gaps, the *lacunae*, between the paragraphs, the sentences, the words, and even the spaces between the letters. Over time, these two foci blended. While we try to learn the author's intent, we also read our own interpretation into the narrative.

I fear we are now coming to a place where the author has no say at all in our cultural narrative, nor does fact. When we read, we no longer take into account the context of the facts presented by the author and the opinion expressed that is based on those facts. Instead, we react based solely on our subjective feeling, and without questioning our feeling.

This is especially true when discussing morals, values, and ethics. I remember a discussion during an ethics class, when several of us felt queasy about a decision made by a particular ethicist. We couldn't pinpoint our anxiety; we just knew that we did not like the decision. We called it our "ooh factor." But a feeling is not a good enough reason upon which to make a responsible decision. We each need to think about our own "ooh factors" and work through them. We must try to understand why we are responding so viscerally. We need to discover the intellectual reason for our reaction rather than merely deliver our own "tyrannical truthiness" as part of our righteous sense of "authority" that comes without reason or knowledge.

Our culture suffers and deteriorates when we revert solely to feelings over rationality, and that deterioration includes religion. Yes, feelings matter, but not to the detriment of reason. "Reason should be the basis for every activity, reflection must come before any undertaking."[123] Unfortunately, reason has been so belittled by the forces of political correctness in our society that we are now falling victim to the feelings of the Left and the Right.

In the twenty-first century, there is no excuse for allowing someone else to interpret the Bible for you. When you give up the obligation to read the Word for yourself, to think about the Word, to discover the meaning, you give away your power, your agency, and your *self* to others—others who could take advantage of you and spread a word that is blasphemous. Every one of us is responsible for our own freedom. The Pharisees taught the doctrine of free will, which Jesus made famous: "You will know the truth and the truth will set you free" (John 8:32). It is our responsibility to "strive to reach God through knowledge and love. God loves [us] to be clear-sighted and out-spoken, not blindly obsequious."[124]

It has crossed my mind that God, in His infinite wisdom, is waiting ever so patiently for His children to reach the place of moral consciousness where He can rest, where every day is the Sabbath, and when He can say, "My children, my children, finally, you see and know." And on that day, He will no longer hide His face from us.

---

[123] Ecclesiasticus 37:16, *The Wisdom of Ben Sira*
[124] Elie Weisel, *Messengers of God*, 91.

XVII
LIVING LIFE IN THE CONTINUOUS PRESENCE OF THE DIVINE

Knock upon yourself as upon a door; and
walk upon yourself as on a straight road. For
if you walk on the road, you cannot get lost . .
. . Open the door for yourself, that you may
know the One who is.

—Elaine Pagels[125]

I was listening recently to a radio program on spirituality. A man was discussing his search for a spiritual home. He had been searching for answers to his spiritual questions but had not yet found a place. He spoke about the moment when he was standing outside, reading a book on Buddhism by the moonlight, looking for a sign that Buddhism was for him. So he looked into the night sky and said, "Give me a sign." Suddenly, a shooting star crossed the sky. That was a sign, he thought, but he still wasn't sure if it was his answer. Years later, he once again found himself outside in the moonlight reading about Buddhism and he made the same request: "Give me a sign." And miraculously, just then a shooting star passed by . . . and he knew: he knew that Buddhism was calling him. The sign was most important for him. "Give me the sign and I will know." No work, no in-depth study, no conscious decision to take Buddhism as his religion or philosophy. Thanks to a shooting star, this man found spirituality in Buddhism.

How sad. How empty. How lazy, to let a random sign make such a crucial life decision. We need to read, to study, and then to critically think about what we've read. Spirituality requires study. Spirituality enters into the heart through the head; from thought to feeling. Unfortunately, "[t]he morality of scholarship as currently

---

125 Pagels, *Revelations*, 101.

practiced, is to encourage everyone to replace difficult pleasures by pleasures universally accessible precisely because they are easier."[126]

Spirituality is "a natural, inherent characteristic common to all humans . . . . It is the intangible, immeasurable, numinous reality that all of us need to find meaning in life and to make life worth living. . . . [It] is the longing for transcendence—the strong desire to experience the feeling of belonging to something larger than ourselves."[127] What was there before the world was created? Where do we come from and where are we going? How can we come to know God?

Spirituality does not exist in a vacuum, nor can it breathe in a heart full of contempt. Our soul connects us to the souls of others and the soul of God through religion, tradition, symbol, ritual, and knowledge. Some people claim that they find spirituality or God in nature, art or poetry, music, meditation, or prayer. But the Spirituality I am talking about is the one connected to, and in a relationship with, God. "When you raise your eyes to heaven, when you see the sun, the moon, the stars-the entire array of heaven—do not be tempted to worship them and serve them" (Deuteronomy 4:19). We connect to the Spirit, to God, through them. They are the connection between the inner and outer, the *nomos* and the *cosmos*. This connection, once made, is ever present. It is a constant sense of wonder and awe, a sense of the child within us, full of imagination, a sense of joy that bubbles up each time you find yourself interacting with the natural world or viewing a piece of art or emotionally overwhelmed by well-written poetry or prose or well-played music.

I remember driving down a backwoods road in early spring. The quiet of that early morning descended on me in slow motion. It took a bit of time before I realized that what I was hearing . . . was silence. My head was filled with silence. The incessant chatter of our modern life had stopped. Hush. This was the true meaning of "the sound of silence." Nothingness. Boundlessness. A sense of a lightness of being. I was aware of nothing, yet of everything. I felt at one with my surroundings. I felt that I was part of all of creation.

---

[126] Harold Bloom, *The Western Canon*, 520.
[127] Somerville, *Imagination*, 7–8.

And I realized that this was a special moment. But it became overwhelming: it was too much, too awesome, too close to the mystery. To live in that place all the time would be to live in a place of unbearable lightness of being. This was a moment of extraordinary revelation of Spirituality, of *Unio Mystica*. But it is not a place in which to remain. It is but a taste of the world to come. To be constantly aware, so close to the *tremendum*, like Moses encountering God on the mountain, would feel like living inside a ball of fire, all-consuming and blinding. Like Moses, we must return to the demands of the present, to this life, to continue to co-create with God. This was my revelation on my road to Damascus.

Today, in our affluent, eminently comfortable, "drive-through" society of personalized self-fulfillment, we like spiritual relativism: designer spirituality, with a small "s" for those who want it all, now, without truly investing anything of themselves. They think they are seekers of truth, but in reality, they are seekers of certainty. They yearn for the absolute yet they end up following the "guru of the month." These gurus are the new "experts," whose life experiences are fodder for the latest self-help tome. These new spiritual leaders turn us away from the God of the Bible, claiming that He represents absolutism, which prevents us from finding our true selves, while they represent "the way," and we should follow their interpretation of life instead of the Bible's.

Paul wrote about the importance of standing on one's spiritual ground in his letter to the Ephesians:

> *So stand your ground, with truth a belt round your waist,*
> *and uprightness a breastplate, wearing for shoes on your feet*
> *the eagerness to spread the gospel of peace and always*
> *carrying the shield of faith.* Ephesians 6:14–15

It is the God of Abraham, the God of Isaac, the God of Jacob, and the God of Jesus, who demands that we follow ethical monotheism and who demands that we exercise our free will. God is the one Spiritual leader who teaches us that we must learn to live in the grey zone, with ambiguity, between the yes and no. Believing in the God of justice and mercy, charity and lovingkindness, requires that we accept as truth that although there is absolute right and wrong, life is more often lived in the grey zone. God provides us with morals, values, and ethics upon which we must base our decisions. These decisions affect the quality of the lives we live as individuals, as well as in community.

There is no shortcut to Spirituality. St. Augustine taught that Spirituality is found through meditation, contemplation, and personal reflection, and that it is through the love of another person that we experience God—because human love has divine love running through it. Elie Wiesel wrote that we reach God through knowledge and love.[128] Martin Buber described relationship with God as "I and Thou." The immanence of God is found in human-to-human relationships as well the relationship between us and God. "Both love of Creator and love of that which he has created are finally one and the same."[129] All relationships require an investment of time and a desire to know the other.

Just as important as the feelings of love as a connection to God, St. Augustine wrote that Scripture is the primary place of encountering God. Scripture is the place where we discover the mystery of God's love and actions and where we find the opportunity for personal transformation. It is in wrestling with God's words that we encounter Him, just as Jacob, wrestling with the angel, encountered God and was transformed. Wrestling with the Word, finding new meaning in old stories, is much the same process as that of a musician taking an old score and bringing new meaning to it while still respecting the composer.

> The pianist is asked to train in sinew and nerve to reproduce with exactitude a score not of his own devising-to maintain fidelity to this text. Yet, this feat is achieved not merely when the technical difficulty of the work is no longer an obstacle, but when the score is thoroughly absorbed that it belongs completely to the performer. The performer then becomes an interpreter and comes at last to share in the inner texture of the relationship with that ineffable other with which the composer was engaged when composing the work.[130]

---

128 Ibid.
129 Martin Buber, *On Judaism*, 209.
130 Atif Rafay, "On the Margins of Freedom," *The Walrus*, April 2011, p. 37, http://thewalrus.ca/ on-the-margins-of-freedom/.

Spirituality is the internalized knowledge that "you are the Temple of God and that the Spirit of God dwells within you."[131] Spirituality, this connection to the sublime, is like a gust of wind, filling all the spaces between the atoms within us with an infusion of lightness, awe, and wonder. It is the sensation of the Holy Spirit, the *Ruach hakodesh*, the instrument of revelation, flowing in, around, and through us, leaving us with a feeling of contentment, of atonement, and a sense of being at one with God and our self.

Sociologists have likened the development of human behavior to looking in a mirror: children mirror what they see. And when that newborn baby first opens her eyes and sees you, her first question is not "Who am I?" Her first question is, "Who are you?"[132] From that moment on, children watch their parents and reflect back the image they observe. And parents do the same with their children. Just as children and parents reflect each other's behavior, humans and God are in a self-reflective relationship. We behave in a way that reflects our understanding of God's behavior, and the Bible is full of descriptions of the changing behaviors of God. At times, God is described as vengeful, full of wrath, a protective warrior, but at other times as merciful, just, charitable, full of loving kindness.

God does not change, though. God is perfection, and there can be no improving on perfection. Our perception of God changes; our need of Him changes and ebbs and flows like in all our relationships. As we learn more about humankind, through physical science and social science, our understanding of all of reality, including God, changes, as it should. Our understanding of life, today, is far different from that of hundreds and thousands of years ago. And our understanding of life and God will change in the future, as it must, because all of creation evolves.

Viewing God as a loving God will lead us to a loving view of ourself and others. "When spiritual joy becomes so intense as to pass onto song and dance, then you have reached the height of service and communion with the divine power."[133] Having happiness within our soul lets us reflect on God with joy and

---

[131] 1 Corinthians 3:16.
[132] Wiesel, *Messengers*, 3.
[133] Agus, *Thought*, 263.

gratitude; this joyful view of Him as a loving God, full of compassion and grace, reflects back on us and fills our soul with lovingkindness. But if we see God as angry, punitive, distant, and uncaring, our soul will shrink, holding on to hurt, pain, and suffering, and refusing to give or receive forgiveness. If we consciously choose to honor God, to praise, extol, glorify, and adore Him, then over time our souls will internalize this God and then compassion for others will become a natural response. We will live mystified by the minutia and magnitude of life, from the smallest particle in the human body to the ever-expanding universe.

Spirituality is about sacred space, sacred place, and sacred time; it is a refuge from chaos. Sacred time allows us to reconnect to our roots: the earth, natural law, the seasons, and the elements. A spiritual time is a time we let go of the profane and the mundane and transport ourselves into a different place, a different space and time. We slow down, externally and internally. The Bible tells us to rest our animals. And we need to rest the animal nature within us, the impulsive and instinctual autonomic nervous system that triggers the stress reaction in the part of our brain called the amygdala. We need to breathe. Inhale the Spirit (the *Ruach*); feel the peace. We need to remind ourselves that simply "being" is enough, and everything else is adornment.

XVIII
HEAL US O LORD,
AND WE SHALL BE HEALED

> *Prayer will not come about by default. It requires education, training, reflection, contemplation. It is not enough to join others; it is necessary to build a sanctuary, brick by brick, within, instants of meditation, moments of devotion. This is particularly true in an age when overwhelming forces seem to conspire at destroying our ability to pray.*
> —Rabbi Abraham J. Heschel[134]

In this life we often face fear and anxiety, sometimes to the point of feeling so overwhelmed that we become paralyzed, unable to make a decision, unable to cope. Our burdens seem too great for us to bear. We call to God to turn His ear to us and pay attention to our cry. Those are the times to envisage the God of compassion and mercy, to imagine putting that burden down at the foot of the Cross and giving it over to the Father, the Son, and the Holy Spirit, even if only for a short time, in order to provide ourselves with a respite—a moment to breathe, to think, to prepare to take on the burden again knowing that God is still beside us.

As a hospital chaplain, I once witnessed a tangible emotional change in the air when a priest was called to provide the sacrament for the sick, prior to surgery. I stood at the end of the bed in the emergency room, the family surrounding their father. There was a palpable sense of fear and anxiety in that small, curtained cubicle. But when the priest placed his vestments over his shoulders, opened his prayer book, and began giving the sacrament, an unbelievable transformation occurred. I felt the hair on my arms

---

[134] Heschel, *Sacred Moments*, 238.

and neck rise, and chills went up and down my spine. And then there was in that little room an unearthly calm, an amazing energy, and a powerful feeling of hope and faith. The peace that suddenly invaded that atmosphere was palpable; powerful; unearthly. It truly felt like the Presence of God came into the room—and all the fear vanished like a mist.

Dr. Herbert Benson, Associate Professor of Medicine at Harvard Medical School and the Deaconess Hospital, has written a book called *Timeless Healing* in which he discusses the effects of religion on healing. He writes that just as we all have hard-wired instincts for flight or fight, and for many of us, an innate fear of heights or snakes, we are also hardwired for God. Human beings, Dr. Benson says, seem to be predisposed to have a need for a connection to something or someone beyond ourselves, something greater than ourselves. Sigmund Freud, on the other hand, was dismissive of religion. He believed that religion derived from our childhood feelings of helplessness; that religion is "an attempt to get control over our sensory-world . . . by means of a wish-world which we have developed as a result of biological and psychological necessities."[135] Dr. Benson disagrees with Freud's negative interpretation of the derivation of religion; he suggests that this predisposed need for religion has been passed down genetically because at some point in human evolution these instincts enabled our survival.

How does belief in God, a higher power, enable survival? Well, we know from medical research that prayer and meditation reduce stress levels, and countless studies have shown that increased stress is physiologically dangerous. We also know that humans suffer from the angst of mortality. But that angst does not stop us from choosing life when faced with death. Perhaps it was faith in God that helped our ancestors deal with the fear of death, by providing a counterbalance so that they would have the courage to carry on. Dr. Benson says that our brains harbor beliefs in a better, nobler meaning to life so that we will not be incapacitated by the acknowledgement and dread of death.[136]

---

[135] *Wisdom of Freud*, 88.
[136] Herbert Benson, *Timeless Healing*, 198.

After reading Dr. Benson's research on prayer and faith helping patients to recover faster, I attended his seminar at Harvard University. Dr. Benson cites from an article written by Dr. Jeffrey S. Levin of Eastern Virginia Medical School: "The mere belief that religion or God is health-enhancing may be enough to produce salutary effects . . . . Various scriptures promise health and healing to the faithful and the physiological effects of expectant beliefs such as this are now documented by mind-body researchers."[137] Jesus is quoted in the Gospels as saying, "Arise, go thy way: thy faith hath made thee whole" (Luke 17:12–19); "receive thy sight; thy faith hath saved thee" (Luke 18:42); "get up, pick up your bed and go off home" (Matthew 9:7). These verses are written as commands; there is no room for ambivalence. There is only the claim that you will become whole again—the power of positive thinking from thousands of years ago.

Prayer circles, or prayer chains, can also affect healing or wholeness (with the understanding that healing does not always mean perfect physical health.) There is great comfort in knowing that one's faith group is praying together to God for your health. "Heal us, O Lord, and we shall be healed: save us and we shall be saved." Communal prayer provides a sense of comfort that results in a reduction of stress and the physiological problems associated with stress. Even when by ourselves, in our sick room, we are not alone. The Holy Spirit is beside us, bringing God's sympathy to the bedside.

Lionel Tiger, author of the 2010 book *God's Brain*, writes that religion can indeed satisfy the most basic yearnings of human beings; this might explain why eighty percent of the world's adults are part of some religious system. Dr. Tiger, a Canadian-born, American-based anthropologist, is the Charles Darwin Professor of Anthropology at Rutgers University and co-Research Director of the Harry Frank Guggenheim Foundation. He is a graduate of McGill University and the London School of Economics at the University of London, England, and a consultant to the U.S. Department of Defense on the future of biotechnology. And as Dr. Tiger says, "You can't have a viable society in which 80% of adults

---

[137] Ibid., 160.

are morons." In other words, the mere existence of five BILLION religious believers around the world shows how foolish is the claim by Daniel Dennett and other neo-atheists that all religious believers are foolish.

The brain can recognize a problem, but it can't always decide what to do about it; religion can help. The two systems work in harmony.[138] Religion, the sacredness of its traditions and rituals and symbols can create what Dr. Tiger refers to as "brainsoothing." Participating in a religious service, people "are in a place and involved in a moment they respect and trust, one from which they leave wiser and better human beings."[139]

The Cognition, Religion and Theology Project, led by Dr. Justin Barrett from the Centre for Anthropology and Mind at Oxford University, was a three-year project ending in 2011 that drew on research from a range of disciplines, including anthropology, psychology, philosophy, and theology. "This project does not set out to prove god or gods exist. Just because we find it easier to think in a particular way does not mean that it is true in fact. If we look at why religious beliefs and practices persist in societies across the world, we conclude that individuals bound by religious ties might be more likely to cooperate as societies." Project co-director professor Roger Trigg, from the University of Oxford's Ian Ramsey Centre, said: "This project suggests that religion is not just something for a peculiar few to do on Sundays instead of playing golf. We have gathered a body of evidence that suggests that religion is a common fact of human nature across different societies."[140]

Charles Darwin had observed, "There can be no doubt that a tribe including many members who from possessing in a high degree the spirit of patriotism, fidelity, obedience, courage and sympathy, were always ready to give aid to each other and to

---

[138] Charles Lewis, "God's Brain: The Neuroscience of Devotion," Holy Post, National Post, March 13, 2010, http://life.nationalpost.com/2010/03/13/gods-brain-the-neuroscience-of-devotion/.

[139] Ibid.

[140] University of Oxford, "Humans 'predisposed' to believe in gods and the afterlife," ScienceDaily, accessed January 8, 2015, www.sciencedaily.com/ releases/ 2011/ 07/ 110714103828.htm.

sacrifice themselves for the common good, would be victorious over most other tribes; and this would be natural selection."[141] These would be the ties that bind one to another. And the root word of religion is *religio*, which means "the ties that bind."

Darwin could not deduce the origin of this altruism. In his words: "The problem, however, of the first advance of savages towards civilization is at present much too difficult to be solved."[142]

At the same time that Darwin was surveying the Galapagos, studying the flora and fauna and developing his theories, the French nobleman Alexis de Tocqueville was traveling through America, studying the revolutionary new society that had evolved there. De Tocqueville discovered that, by keeping religion separate from the State, the Americans were enabling religion to be more influential than one would have thought. Religion was influential in America *because* of the separation of Church and State: *because* religion never got directly involved in politics and vice versa. De Tocqueville discovered that religious leaders in the 1830s were heavily involved in strengthening families, building communities, and starting charities. They inspired people to a sense of the common good, educating them in "habits of the heart," and giving them what he called "their apprenticeship in liberty." He wrote, "In the United States religion exercises but little influence on the laws and the details of public opinion but it directs the customs of the community and by regulating domestic life it regulates the state."[143]

Politics and ethics—of rights and responsibilities, initiative and cooperation that—enable a country to continue to develop common shared stories, beliefs, values, and priorities. History shows that these are the nations that thrive: ones that care for the stranger, the other, the weak and the poor, the widow and the orphan. Nations that thrive are those that include religion in the public square.

The Divine Will can only be illumined by the Divine Light

---

[141] Rabbi Jonathan Sacks, "Biblical Insights into the Good Society," Ebor Lecture 2011, presented at York St. John University, York, England, November 30, 2011, http://www.rabbisacks.org/biblical-insights-into-the-good-society-ebor-lecture-2012/.
[142] Ibid., as quoted by Rabbi Sacks.
[143] Ibid.

within the human soul: the double light of intelligence and conscience.[144]

I have found that my connection to God fluctuates. It is always greater during time of extreme joy and deepest sorrow. Perhaps at these moments my feelings are so profound as to be indescribable to another; too strong, too overwhelming, too all-encompassing to share with a friend or family member. But I experience great comfort from sharing these times with God, who has been with me from the beginning and will be with me at the end.

My work as a chaplain at Toronto General Hospital included caring for those waiting for heart transplants. Some waited for many months. Everything that they did or ate was recorded: even the number of grapes, because grapes contain fluid and fluid intake had to be strictly monitored. Finally, a heart became available for one of my patients whom I had been seeing regularly. His family was overjoyed. But, after the surgery, this gentleman was unbearably depressed. His wife and children could not understand why. After all, he had just been given a gift, and the greatest gift. They were struggling emotionally because they had believed that he would be ecstatic over his new lease on life, that he would be completely healed and then finally come home.

I, too, was at a loss. Then I learned that there were biological reasons for the depression, having to do with brain chemicals. The biological part of the depression could be helped with drugs. But there were spiritual issues, too. This man was burdened by the knowledge that, for him to live, to come home to his loved ones, someone had had to die.

It is very difficult to wish death on someone else in order to receive their heart, and to know that their family will now be in mourning. Such a traumatic situation can make the recipient heartsick. How does one rationalize the death of one to save another? I don't think it is possible. I don't think one can ease this type of pain through logic. When psycho-social sciences and medicine can't heal, though, religion can help. I have yet to find a medical term that deals with forgiveness, especially forgiveness of

---

[144] Agus, *Jewish Thought*, 6.

oneself, first, for having prayed or wished for the death of another. Yet a belief in a forgiving God makes the process possible.

Jill Bolte Taylor, a neuro-anatomist and the author of *My Stroke of Insight*, wrote that her stroke led her to observe the physical and neurological workings of the two halves of the brain. They work synergistically, yet "see" the world differently. She described the left brain as the "doing-consciousness." It is the repository of detail, of analytical judgement, of categorizing and thinking in language. The left brain makes sense of the external world, providing boundaries and a sense of self differentiated from others. The right brain exists only in the present moment. It is "spontaneous, carefree, and imaginative."[145] The right brain perceives the big picture. It is the repository of the sense of oneness with the vastness of the universe.[146] The right brain contains "the being-consciousness."[147] One side of the brain is closely connected to science, the other to God.

In the Bible there are two stories about the "birth" of Adam. In Genesis 1:26 God said, "Let us make man in our image, in the likeness of ourselves, and let them be masters of the fish of the sea, the birds of heaven, the cattle, all the wild animals and all the creatures that creep along the ground." The second story comes from Genesis 2:7: "Yahweh God shaped man from the soil of the ground and blew the breath of life into his nostrils, and man became a living being."

Adam version 1 is the master of all he sees. His job is to subdue the land, to conform it to his needs. He will face life head on, open and curious to all things. He is the first scientist. He will "do." Adam version 2 is different. He was made from the land, from *adam*: "earth." He is part of nature, not the master of it. He is enthralled with all of creation because of his connection to the ground beneath him. He felt the presence of God when God breathed life into His nostrils. Now he wonders, "Who is this who breathed life into me?" Adam version 2 wants to understand his

---

145 Jill Bolte Taylor, *My Stroke of Insight*, 29–32.
146 Taylor, *Insight*, 67.
147 Ibid., 71.

place in the universe and his connection to all that is. He wants to understand the big picture and his place of "being" in the universe.

Like the "doing-consciousness" of the left brain and the "being-consciousness" of the right brain that come together to form one brain, the two personalities of Adam come together in each of us—the doing and the being—calling us both to science and to God.[148]

---

[148] Concept taken from *The Lonely Man of Faith*, by Rabbi Joseph Soloveitchik.

XIX
THE GOSPEL OF STORYTELLING

Why did God create mankind?
Because God likes stories.

—Rabbi Jonathan Sacks

Science and religion are not polar opposites. They each have a place in our understanding of ourselves and the world in which we live. Bible stories, in some ways, expose and explain human behavior better than the psycho-social sciences can, because Bible stories are universal, plus they speak to the entirety of the human condition. Albert Einstein explained it this way: "Science without religion is lame. Religion without science is blind."

In my work as a chaplain, I can hear my patients' concerns through their stories and then assist them with pastoral terms like shame, guilt, grace, forgiveness, or repentance. Concepts like *animus* and *anima*, ego, id, and super-ego make no human connection at all, but stories soothe our souls. I have come to believe (with apologies to Descartes), "I speak, therefore I am," not "I think, therefore I am."

Science without religion is lame.
Religion without science is blind.

—Albert Einstein

Charles Darwin observed two different components of expression in animals and humans. One is the objective expression that is seen in both animals and man. It is the visible change in expression, as well as changes in physiology, as a result of a particular experience, such as fear. It is an automatic, unconscious response of the body, controlled by the reptilian part of the brain known as the amygdala. But in man there is also another reaction: an internal, personal one that is subjective. It is the person's emotional response to the event. Neuroscientists such as Antonio

Damasio, a professor at the University of Southern California (whom I mentioned in chapter seven), have now found markers (patterns of nerve cell activity) in the brain for things we see, as well as markers in the brain for feelings that are produced by what we see.[149] Dr. Herbert Benson, cardiologist and associate professor of Medicine at Harvard University, noted that in the brain there is a "complex system in which patterns of nerve cell activation are created and stored, and in which life experiences mingle with genetics, constantly shifting the cellular pathways and determining all our thoughts, movements, feelings and functions."[150]

Dr. Jill Bolte Taylor summarizes patterns of human thought this way: we think about something and so activate our thought circuitry; we experience a feeling as a result of that thought, for example joy or sorrow, and thus trigger our emotional circuitry; we then have a physiological response to that feeling, like increased blood pressure, and this triggers our physiological circuitry; and then we act out the thought in our behavior, which uses our multidimensional circuitry.[151]

Pascal Boyer, a professor of memory at Washington University in St. Louis, wrote about the difference between episodic memories—a one-time event—and mental time travel memories— MTT—which come closer to reliving the entire experience. Our memories of events are triggered or recalled by familiar sights, smells, or sounds, and as our emotions are connected to visceral experiences in the brain, we relive the feelings. Kelly Lambert, professor of neuroscience at Randolph-Macon College calls these recollections "full body and brain memories."[152]

Rabbi Jonathan Sacks wrote: "Judaism's greatness is that it gave space to both prophet and priest, to inspirational figures on the one hand, and on the other, daily routines . . . that take exalted visions

[149] Bruce Charlton, review of *The Feeling of What Happens: Body, Emotion and the Making of Consciousness,* 1999, http:// www.hedweb.com/ bgcharlton/ damasioreview.html.

[150] Benson, *Timeless Healing,* 197.

[151] Jill Bolte Taylor, *My Stroke of Insight,* 163.

152 Kelly Lambert, "Santa on the Brain," New York Times, December 22, 2013, http:// www.nytimes.com/ 2013/12/22/ opinion/ sunday/ santa-on-the-brain.html? page wanted = all.

and turn them into patterns of behavior that reconfigure the brain and change how we feel and who we are."[153]

We humans can remember the same feelings without having to relive the same experience. Because our internal world is a world of emotion, and our thoughts and emotions are linked so tightly together, we can think ourselves into a state of fear or anxiety from ghost stories, or calmness and joy from prayer or meditation. More than 2000 years ago, Jesus understood the connection between thought and emotion. He preached against harboring sinful thoughts even if those thoughts did not lead to action. We now know that having sinful, or negative thoughts, can trigger negative emotions and anxiety. Dr. Taylor writes that we "have the power to consciously choose which emotional or physiological loops" we want to experience.[154]

Dr. Damasio says that awareness of our inner states evolved so that we could use emotions to evaluate external perceptual information, the things that we learn from the five senses. Two things are simultaneously being laid down in the brain in working memory: what we perceive, and the corresponding feelings. Those feelings, those emotions, are essential to rational thought. Whether we actually, phenomenally, experience an event or experience it vicariously through the actions of others or seeing movies or reading, we still lay down messages in that part of the brain that deals with emotion.

Many of us believe that only rational thought is involved in decision-making. Neuro-imaging studies, though, show that tasks involving moral judgement not only activate rational thought but also may activate brain areas known to process emotion. Because we use thought as well as emotion to evaluate what we experience personally or vicariously, the stories we read and the values they teach us will affect our brain.[155]

[153] Rabbi Jonathan Sacks, "Sprints and Marathons," Chabad.org, http://www.chabad.org/ parshah/ article_cdo/ aid/ 2527513/ jewish/ Sprints-Marathons.htm.
[154] Taylor, My Stroke of Insight, 163.
[155] Bruce Charlton, review of The Feeling of What Happens, http:// www.hedweb.com/ bgcharlton/damasioreview.html.

In an earlier chapter, I wrote about God hardening the heart of Pharaoh when Moses asked him to let the Jewish people go. Jewish tradition says that God hardened Pharaoh's heart because He did not want Pharaoh to be able to claim that he let the Israelites go in a moment of emotional weakness. God wanted Pharaoh to think through his decision, rationally and unemotionally. Based on Dr. Damasio's findings, Pharaoh's moral decision-making did contain an emotional component. And that emotional component would have come from experiences and stories that had laid down markers in his brain. What experiences and stories could have led him to deny the Israelites the right to freedom? Here are some: He lived in a society that valued its gods more than its people. He lived at a time when human beings were worked harder than beasts of burden. He lived at a time when his orders to murder the male children of a group of immigrants were obeyed by almost all of his subjects.

According to these scientific theories, it seems that how we exercise free will can be taught. If we choose to make the stories of the Bible *our* stories, then we will learn and internalize the importance of nurturing moral discernment and free will. Free will may be a naturally occurring process (think of Adam and Eve), but maintaining Western culture requires that we continue to teach the ethics and values of the Bible. We must teach this ethic as a firewall, a bulwark against cultures and religions that are stuck in the past, that fear change and free will, or that promote extreme submission. Those cultures hold on to ideas that are albatrosses around their necks, preventing them from growing and adapting to a changing world, because their beliefs are written in stone and just as dead.

Wilhelm von Humboldt said, in the eighteenth century, "Language is, as it were, the external manifestation of the minds of the peoples. Their language is their soul, and their soul is their language."[156] In the twentieth century, Roland Barthes wrote; "Man does not exist prior to language, either as a species or an individual. We never find a state where man is separated from language, which

---

[156] Wilhelm von Humboldt, "Humboldt: 'on Language': On the Diversity of Human Language Construction and Its Influence on the Mental Development of the Human Species," https:// www.goodreads.com/ work/ quotes/ 346887-ber-die-verschiedenheit-des-menschlichen-sprachbaues-und-ihren-einfluss.

he then creates in order to 'express' what is taking place within him: it is language which teaches the definition of man, not the reverse."[157] More recently, poet Muriel Rukeyser wrote: "The universe is made of stories, not atoms,"[158] and religion plays an important role in the stories we hear, believe and internalize.

For more than 2000 years, generations of people in the Western world have been raised on stories from the Bible. When I went to school there were two systems, Catholic and public. The public schools were called Protestant. I was neither. We read Bible stories every day, not for a particular view of religion or a particular dogma but for the values that were considered vital to all citizens of all races, colors, creeds, and religions living in this Western culture. These stories became part of the collective consciousness of society. They informed our collective will. They became part of our shared education, memories, culture, ideals, and expectations. My children's generation and their children do not seem to have these shared stories. They are unfamiliar with them, as well as with most of the classics of the Western canon.

What will replace these stories? What will be the collective consciousness of our children? What will be the basis for a consensus required to run a democracy? For those who constantly berate religion as the cause of all evil, what common shared stories are they offering as its replacement?

> *Deprive children of stories and you leave them unscripted, anxious stutterers in their actions as in their words.*[159]
>
> —Alasdair MacIntyre

The stories of the Bible are not perfect. Western culture is not perfect. But as we become more diverse, we need a shared morality that protects and promotes freedom, free will, individuality, and

---

[157] Mark Neuman, *Self, Sign, and Symbol* (Lewisburg, PA: Bucknell University Press, 1987), 160.

[158] Muriel Rukeyser, as quoted on Storyteller.net, http:// www.storyteller.net/ articles/ 160.

[159] Alasdair MacIntyre, *After Virtue*, 1981, quoted by Rabbi Jonathan Sacks in "A Nation of Storytellers," http:// www.chabad.org/ parshah/ article_cdo/ aid/2657257/ jewish/ A-Nation-of-Storytellers.htm.

care for the community. If not the ethics and values of the God of the Bible, what shared morality will it be?

XX
THE GARDEN OF EDEN

And the Lord God planted a garden eastward in Eden; and there He put the man whom He had formed.

Genesis 2:8

On the sixth day, God created man and woman: not from an utterance, not from a word, but from His hands and His breath; we are created in His image, capable of reason, moral thinking, and free will. He created Adam and Eve, the first children, the first of His children. And He placed them in the lush Garden of Eden. And He told them to eat and enjoy all that was before them in the Garden of Eden, all but the fruit of the Tree of Knowledge of Good and Evil. That tree—right there in the middle of the garden. That sensual tree with luscious fruit. That tree. Don't eat from that tree.

But, like all children, the admonishment not to eat piqued their curiosity, their childishness, and their innocence. How could they not try the fruit? It's not as if it were hidden in a corner of the garden behind a fence. It was right there. In front of them. So easy to access. So forbidden. It is too much to bear. And the first children that ate of the fruit now exist in all of us, as does the first breath that created us all.

Then God called out. "Where are you?"

"Adam, where are you?" is a question from God. But God is omnipotent, omniscient, and omnipresent. It is a rhetorical question, for God certainly knew the whereabouts of the physical presence of Adam. But that was not the intent of the question.

God was asking, "Where are you emotionally and spiritually? From the beginning we have been together. There are no boundaries between you and Me and all that I set before thee. But something has happened. You no longer rely on me nor follow My lead. So the time has come for you and Eve to leave this place, this Garden, your first home. But know this: you will return to Me, to your Source, and I will be waiting for you to embrace you with My boundless love. And we will be together as before."

We naturally bemoan the expulsion of Adam and Eve from the Garden of Eden. Had they not disobeyed God's commandment not to eat of the fruit of the tree of knowledge, we would all be living in paradise. And the story of the human journey would have ended. But they chose to eat of the fruit and condemned—or gifted—all of us with free will.

True atonement comes only at the end of life when our energies unite. The melting of me with the energy of the world is to become one with the universe. My soul will join with the souls of others and with God, the infinite energy. Our desire for atonement begins at birth, when we are expelled from our mother's womb. We are torn from the oneness of mother and child where all our needs had been met. We had eaten without swallowing. We had breathed without inhaling. We had floated in warm water, swaying gently with the movements of our mother, embraced by her. We were as one, attached to each other. We depended on her. She had made all the decisions for our well-being. And then, without warning, we felt the walls closing in, suffocating us. We were being pushed, pulled, and squeezed. Birth separated us from that oneness, in an instant, when the umbilical cord was cut, just as Adam and Eve were escorted out from the Garden of Eden and were separated for the first time from God, their life source. Just as we were cut from our oceanic connection with our mother in a nanosecond, separated from her, our source of life, in order to begin a life separate from her, so we were cut off from the Garden of Eden, a place of oceanic limitlessness, a merging of boundaries where one cannot see the other because one is with the other, part of the other. And we are sent on a journey to find and create our "self."

But with the expulsion comes a yearning to return to that safe place. It is a yearning that follows us all of our lives, a desire to return to the Source.

For many of us, our lives are spent searching and yearning for a reconnection, a desire to be at-one with another—whether with a spouse, with a parent, or with God. We search for atonement, peace, and forgiveness. Spirituality is that search for that reconnection, a return to something about which we have some vague memory, some slim knowledge, undefined but palpable. And the same yearning we have for the ineffable reveals itself in our yearning to re-experience the sense of joy and comfort—real or imagined—from our past. This is the same yearning that is tapped in Spirituality and nostalgia; it is the need to feel connected to something and someone beyond ourselves—because we are not meant to be alone.

According to Socrates and Plato, the human psyche, or soul, is separate from the body; it existed before the birth of the body and it will exist after the death of the body. Socrates taught that we each have an authentic knowledge within us, and by thinking deeply about the meaning of life, this knowledge will come to light; we will be en-lightened. He described this knowledge as the recollection of an insight that we had forgotten.[160]

The rabbis tell a story about the soul as it is about to enter into the body of a baby on the cusp of birth. They tell us that the soul is filled with all the knowledge of God, Wisdom, and the Word, revealed to us through a light that is shown to each soul before it enters the world. It is the same light that those who have returned from death tell of seeing.[161] But the baby's soul does not want to enter the body and leave the Oneness. So an angel gently kisses the baby between the nose and lips, to take away all that knowledge, all the meaning of life. Thus, the baby enters the world empty of that knowledge but always yearning for it, searching for it, all her life.

The mark of the angel's kiss, in the crease between the nose and the lips, is the ever-present reminder that, just as we are all still spiritually and emotionally connected to our mother after the separation of the umbilical cord, we are all still connected to God through the divine spark placed within us. It is through this divine

160 Armstrong, *Transformation*, 260.
161 Lawrence Kushner, *Honey from the Rock*, 100.

spark that we will become one with Him when we return to the Source of all creation.

XXI
WANDERING IN THE DESERT:
FROM SLAVERY TO FREEDOM

*We can easily forgive a child who is afraid of
the dark;
the real tragedy of life is when men are afraid
of the light.*

—Plato

In the 1990s I had my first appointment with a psychiatrist. I had such severe anxiety that I was sometimes frozen in place. I was all revved up but with nowhere to go. My anxiety attacks felt like internal earthquakes, jostling me with knots of steel; I felt trapped in a net of panic. In such a place, choosing a path is difficult; I wanted to go in one direction but was paralyzed by fear and held back by feet of clay. We live in a culture that teaches us that we have the right to choose, to make our own decisions about anything. But sometimes the ability to choose is just not there. My doctor did his best to help me, to keep me from making a decision that could come back to haunt me. I was so scared that I knew I would not be back to see him, and he knew it too. As I was leaving for that last time, he said to me, "You are taking a flight away from freedom. Now is not the time to leave." I was on the edge of a revelation that would free me from my anxiety, but I couldn't face it. I ran; back to my comfort zone. I had no idea at the time, but I was replaying the behavior of the Israelites from thousands of years ago.

The story of Moses leading the Israelites out of Egypt, out of slavery, can be read as a metaphor for the struggles and fears many of us face in our lives. The Israelites had crossed the Sea of Reeds and were safe in the desert. But it wasn't long before the complaints began. They were frightened. Where would they get food, water, or basic shelter? So they began to wax poetic about the past, viewing it through discolored glasses. Egypt had not been so bad. At least there they had food and shelter and a bed in which to sleep. Nostalgia through the lens of fear can lead to a flight from the freedom that is waiting for you: a new life, with more choices. Instead, we turn back to "the comfort of the enslavement of the known and familiar,[162] whether the familiar is a reclusive life, an abusive relationship, or a stifling job.

I was living with the same fear as the Israelites, who could not face the future because of their fear of freedom. There is a strange comfort with the familiar, even when the familiar is uncomfortable. The Israelites had no understanding of the meaning of *free will* nor how to put it into practice in their lives. Their free will had been lost in the generations of enslavement and incarceration. God soon realized that the Israelites, enslaved for so long, were afraid to move forward to freedom. But God stood by His people. "By day in a pillar of cloud to show them the way, and by night in a pillar of fire to give them light. . . . The pillar of cloud never left its place ahead of the people during the day, nor the pillar of fire during the night" (Exodus 13:21–22). God was a constant companion: leading them, carrying them, and providing all the necessities of life, guiding them until they could stand on their own.

In 2009, I was back in therapy. This time, my therapist was a psychoanalyst. Unlike psychiatry or other talk therapies, in psychoanalysis you lie on a couch, facing a wall, while your therapist sits behind you, listening and writing. There is a logical reason for that set-up. It's like going to a drive-in movie, with one person sitting in the driver's seat and the passenger sitting in the back seat. The movie unfolds on the screen in front and the two people watch it together and then discuss it. With psychoanalysis, you're the driver and the analyst is the back seat passenger. Although you are facing a wall and talking to it, you are projecting your story onto that blank "screen" through your words. The analyst is visualizing your story. Then, together, you discuss it, analyze it, critique it, and question it, looking for multiple meanings, as if it were great literature. The idea is that through talking, the two of you will uncover the problem. The revelation that comes from

---

162 Erich Fromm, *You Shall Be as Gods*, 99.

the psychoanalytic experience will hopefully free you from behaviors that are preventing you from living your life.

Some journeys are too difficult to face alone. When God revealed His teachings to the people at Mount Sinai, the people were terrified, "seeing the thunder pealing, the trumpet blasting and the mountain smoking" (Exodus 20:18–19). At the moment of the most important revelation, a revelation that would free them from the past and reveal to them a new way of living, they backed away. They were afraid. It was overwhelming. They couldn't face it and they couldn't deal with the entire revelation at one time. So they turned to Moses to help them, to talk to them, to take away their fear.

Later in the story, Moses left his people to ascend the mountain at Mount Sinai. Moses gave instructions to them to wait, to prepare for his return. Once he was out of sight, though, it was as if he were lost to them. How long should we wait for his return? How long can we wait? How will we cope without our leader to hold our hands? What if he does not return? For me, the "loss" of Moses represents the loss of our sense of self, of the ability to make a plan and implement it. So, out of fear of making a decision, we exchange one authority for another. We find another external authority to tell us what to do and, over time, we give up any new-found freedom to this new idol, just as the Israelites did when they built the Golden Calf, into which they put all their possessions, material and spiritual. They gave up everything of themselves and put it into the idol, into an object that could not move, hear, speak, feel, or help them. The Golden Calf represents fear and paralysis and the loss of personal freedom. The Israelites, at that moment in time, were a symbol of the need in each of us for assistance. The Israelites needed Moses and God.

We all need a hand up, at some time in our lives. Today, some ask, will it be science or religion? For me, I have two hands with which to reach out for support: one holding on to science (my analysts), the other to religion (God).

XXII
MISFORTUNE LIES HEAVY

Misfortune lies heavy upon anyone who does not know what the outcome will be.

Ecclesiastes 8:6

Fill your time to whatever extent you can by learning about things divine, not simply to know them but also to do them; and when you shut your book, observe around you, see within you, to know by your hand you can make into a deed something that has been learned.

—Moses of Ereux

In the year 2000, I went into hospital for minor surgery—and a week later came out with a colostomy bag. The purpose of that surgery had been to remove a cyst from one of my ovaries. It isn't a big deal, relatively speaking. Never think of surgery as minor, though. In my case, the doctor had unknowingly perforated my bowel. By the time I had my check up, four days later, there was quite a soupy, bacterial mess in my abdomen. When the surgeon, surgeon number two, opened me up, he had to resection part of my bowel. He cut it and removed the unhealthy section, clamped off one end, and brought the other end out my left side and attached it to a bag.

When it came time to go home, I had to put on street clothes. But I had this bag attached to me. I didn't know what to wear. How would my pants fit over the bag? My youngest daughter went out to buy new loose-fitting pants for me, with a waistband that I could adjust. When I went to get dressed, though, I fell apart. Where do I put the bag? Does it go inside my underwear or outside? Do I need different underwear to hold the bag? When the bag fills up, will it show through my clothes? Of all the things I had experienced in my life, how to dress in this situation brought me to my knees. My eldest daughter was living in New York and calling me all the time. It was her wry sense of humor that put all in perspective. So, Mom, she said; do you match your shoes or your dress to your bag? And so it began.

Then, just as I was recovering from my emergency surgery, I was rushed back in for more. I had developed sepsis. I was being poisoned by my own body. At this point I was physically, mentally, emotionally, and spiritually bankrupt. I had never thought of myself as someone who gives up so easily. I don't know if I had lost hope or that I was just exhausted from the marathon of the unexpected. I told my surgeon—surgeon number three—that this surgery was it. No more. I have a very high pain threshold, but I had long passed the high end of the scale. My surgeon told me, unequivocally, that I would go through as many surgeries as necessary to get me back to health. She proudly told me of a patient who had required thirteen surgeries. I wasn't impressed. If two surgeries were overwhelming, thirteen were inconceivable. It was not one of my finer moments.

But I began to understand the true depths of depression, the kind that leads to thoughts of suicide. As King David said, "My strength was trickling away, my bones were all disjointed, my heart was turning to wax, melting inside me" (Psalm 22:14). After the surgery, I was left with a sensation of emotional emptiness, hopelessness, of being a burden—and not just physically. I wanted out. I knew that caring for someone with extreme depression is exhausting, and who wants to be the one to exhaust the ones you love? More than any of the other emotions I had to endure, it was my sense of helplessness that I found most devastating. No way out. No end to the pain.

Major surgery certainly leaves the patient with physical pain: the kind that starts at the toes and screams up the legs and throughout the whole body from inside out and steals your free will, your ability to think clearly and choose life; pain that brings thoughts of death and quickly erases the memories that make life worth living; pain, the devil, the serpent in the Garden, tempting you to eat of the fruit of death. And there is mental pain: the total lack of control over your life, because some other force has taken over.

Suicide is the ultimate act of control, the ultimate expression of the desire for order. In the mind of the one who wants to die, it is a well-thought-out, justified act of selflessness. My loved ones will be fine, I told myself. This way I won't become a burden to them. Suicide comes to symbolize peace. It all seems so normal. Except that the one considering suicide is suffering from an illness so overwhelming that her decision making ability is not functioning properly. I was, at that moment, mentally ill.

Looking back over my life, I can see that depression had been my constant companion. But, like a fish in water, you don't realize it until you are out of it. And there is a big difference between *being depressed* and *depression*. To be depressed is to experience a deep sadness, but one that usually has an underlying cause, like the death of a friend or of a lifelong dream. Sometimes grief can become unmanageable and morph into depression, but often, a state of *being depressed* that is based on an event can be remedied quite quickly with psychotherapy and perhaps medication. Depression is different. It is heavy. It is mind-numbing. It is exhausting. It feels like Atlas looks, carrying the troubles of the world on your shoulders. Mine stalked me stealthily, like a creature of the night, waiting patiently for the right moment to seep inside me, without warning, then enveloping me in darkness that got progressively heavier. I lost all feeling. I didn't care about anything. No highs, no lows, just indifference.

I was once told a metaphor that compared life to a tree. What do you think about trees, I was asked? I said that I loved them. I especially love trees in autumn. I was then asked if the tree had to do anything for me to admire the tree. No. So, if you can love a tree for being a tree, why can't you love yourself for just being you? Good question. I suggested, though, that as much as I loved a tree, if I were a tree I would want to be home to a nest of birds or squirrels. I would want a purpose. I was not at the point emotionally where my intrinsic value as a human being, as a child of God, was going to be enough for me to keep going. Secular scientific wisdom presented by sociologists, psychologists, and psychiatrists could not give me sufficient purpose in life to make me want to stay alive.

While I did receive help from the psycho-social sciences, it was my religion that sustained me. One might ask why the love of and for my family—my widowed mother, my three children—was not enough to keep me here. I have no answer. I am grateful, though, that I had one more resource to turn to for help: I reached out to my rabbi. I remember driving to the synagogue, exhausted. Everything at that time was exhausting. I went to see him in his book-lined office. We sat across from each other at a large desk strewn with books. I think he is younger than I am, but his experiences in pastoral care and as a teacher gave him wisdom beyond his years. When I think back, I picture a dark room, but I think it was more that I was in a dark place. I had been attending synagogue services and classes regularly for some time, so he knew of my love of study, of parsing Bible stories and searching out the meaning. I remember being taught that we don't make meaning, rather we merely find it, because God has provided all the meaning already.

My rabbi upheld me by tapping into the part of me that is deeply connected to God. He reminded me that as a child of God, I do not have the right to take my own life. I am obligated to "choose life for you and your children." He said that the most important thing I could do was to study God's teachings. He gave me reason to live, while taking away any thought of taking my own life. Just read a few sentences a day, perhaps a prayer, he said.

I now had a purpose. Study. Stay alive.

> These are the things of which a person enjoys the fruits in this world, while the principal remains in the hereafter, namely; honoring father and mother, practice of kindness, hospitality to strangers, visiting the sick, dowering the bride, attending the dead to the grave . . . but study of Torah exceeds them all.[163]

There was comfort and relief in my rabbi's message. His words, his compassion, his reference to the Biblical commandment to choose life as the greatest of all commandments, and that Bible study, something that was dear to me, lifted the burden from my

---

[163] Handler, Hetherington, and Kelman, *Give Me Your Hand*, 11.

shoulders. I was no longer in a state of anxiety over whether to choose between life and death. My deep depression did not lift right away, but talking to my rabbi gave me hope. It was as if I had been holding my breath and now I could breathe again.

One would think that I could have helped myself: after all, I was a trained chaplain. There is a story about Rabbi Chanina who was ill. So his friend, Rabbi Yochanan, visited him. When Rabbi Chanina complained about his suffering, Rabbi Yochanan suggested to him that he tell himself the same words of comfort that he had given to others. Rabbi Chanina responded: "When I was free of sufferings, I could help others; but now that I am myself a sufferer, I must ask others to help me." What do we learn from this story? When we are ill, we need to reach out to others. And we must learn both how to give and take aid graciously.

The healing of my soul could begin because I was no longer in fear of losing it. It was for me, I think, the same feeling of relief that my Christian patients expressed to me when I encouraged them to visualize laying their burdens down at the foot of the Cross. I turned to my God to help me, to take away my fear. I read. I studied. I prayed to the God of my ancestors.

> My God, the soul You have placed within me is pure; You created it, fashioned it, and breathed it into me. You constantly safeguard it for me and eventually You will take it from me to be restored only in the hereafter. Yet, as long as it is within me I will gratefully give thanks to You, O Lord, in Whose Hands are **the souls of all the living.**[164]

My rabbi continued to provide spiritual care for me. Six months later, when it was time for me to return to the hospital for surgery to, hopefully, reverse the colostomy, he came to the hospital and prayed with me. This time, I feared dying. I had come full circle. I am blessed with wonderful friends who care for me when I am in distress. But something profoundly different takes place when the prayers of our ancestors are recited by a learned, empathic rabbi or

---

[164] "The Art of Jewish Prayer," Jewish Healing, http:// www.jewishealing.com/ JewishPrayer.html.

pastor. My rabbi brought with him the feeling of the presence of God.

So many people today turn to self-help books and gurus who claim they have the answers to our deepest, most profound feelings. They are merely attempting to fill the vacuum left by the presumed absence of religion. Religion and its teachings provide outlets for our minds and souls, and opportunities for accepting failure and moving forward. Emotions need a place to be. If a feeling like anger, guilt, or shame has nowhere to go, no outlet, it will be repressed. Religion has rituals and traditions that help us deal with those emotions. Religion provides the language and the path; words such as revelation, repentance, forgiveness, redemption, atonement, and resurrection, and rituals like the Eucharist, prayer, study, and throwing bread into the water to scatter the past and cleanse it of its control.

A good friend of mine, Cathy, gave me a sign that I put up on my wall during my recovery. It was a quote from Isaiah 41:10: "So do not fear, for I am with you; do not be dismayed, for I am your God. I will strengthen you and help you; I will uphold you with my righteous right hand." Cathy had been at my side when I was rushed back in for my second emergency surgery. She is a devoutly spiritual Catholic, so she stood by my bed, placed her hands on me, and prayed for me in the name of Jesus. And calmness came over me. And I knew that I was loved, by Cathy and by God. What makes this so special is that Cathy and I were raised in different religions. I am Jewish. But I knew that her prayers for me came from a special place deep within her soul, reaching out to mine. We three were connected: God, Cathy, me.

Of the three weeks I was in the hospital, I spent two of them completely on IV, taking no food or liquids into my stomach. It is difficult to maintain weight, let alone gain weight, when you can't eat or drink. By the third week, I was diagnosed with failure to thrive. Bowel surgery requires that one not eat or drink until the doctor can be sure that the bowel is working. The signal is the ability to pass gas.

There I was, lying in bed in the iconic blue hospital gown that never fits or covers what it is supposed to cover, hooked up to an

IV drip, a morphine drip, and attached to a catheter which was hanging over the bed for all to see. I had drains sticking out of my sides and, of course, my colostomy bag. Can you imagine lying in bed and praying to pass gas? My entire worldview was focused on this one simple biological act that we all take for granted and actually are embarrassed by: unexpected puffs of wind. All my energy, all my thoughts, every ounce of my being was focused on willing my bowel to work.

Several times a day a nurse would come into my room, place her stethoscope on my belly, and listen intently. She was searching for the growl in my bowel that would let her know that the healing process had begun. I would lie very still, holding my breath to prevent any ambient sound. She would close her eyes and move the stethoscope around, searching for signs of life. It reminded me of other days long past when my obstetrician would place his stethoscope on my belly, also searching for signs of life. Each day I would concentrate on my bowel, willing it to grumble or rumble, or even whimper, to give me any sign that it was rising out of its slumber.

For every event that we experience, we can choose our response. God said, "I have given you the blessing and the curse, life and death: choose life." We can choose to be active participants in our lives, choose to live, or we can choose to be angry victims of circumstance, and so wither.

I chose not only to survive, but to thrive. It wasn't an overnight decision. I had to deal with physical and mental pain. There is a Jewish prayer that is said in the morning that became my mantra:

> Blessed are You, O Lord, King of the Universe, who has fashioned us with wisdom combining veins, arteries, and vital organs in a finely balanced network. It is clear that if one of them were ruptured or blocked it would be impossible to stand before You. Blessed are You, O Lord, who heals all flesh and does wondrous things.

I continued to say this prayer and acknowledge to myself that I had always taken my health for granted. Or, if not for granted, I just never gave it a second thought. There I would be, each morning, lying in bed and I would begin this prayer knowing that I am speaking to my God, lying down because God was right: you cannot stand before Him when your pipes aren't working.

Feelings and emotions are morally neutral. There are no good or bad feelings. There are only healthy and unhealthy responses to them. God gave us the same emotions that He exhibits, and they all serve a purpose. There is a time for every feeling under heaven. The surgery brought out all kinds of anger in me. But anger can keep you alive when all else has failed. It can give you a reason for living.

I remember some of my darkest days when I held on to my anger, the way children cling to their teddy bears. I would replay all the experiences that had caused me pain, both mental and physical. They became my lullabies. My anger was the one emotion that kept me going, and I clung to it like a drowning woman. My anger was my connection to life. But there comes a time when anger no longer has a place inside. Anger is never pretty, and it is all consuming. It needs a place to go. Some of my patients had been full of anger. Usually towards God. Some of them felt guilty for being angry with God. I used to tell them that it is okay to be angry with God, because it means that you are still in a relationship with Him. And I told my patients that as long as you are in a relationship, you are still choosing to be alive. How much better it is to scream and rage against God than against another person. How much better it is to scream at God than to dwell in silence.

When we withhold rage, we turn it inward and so eat ourselves alive. We edit what we say, what we do, what we think. We become experts in emotional constipation while we suffocate our souls. And when we finally explode with rage and anger, we turn our emotions into a misplaced desire for vengeance. But if we tell ourselves that vengeance belongs to God, we can, over time, let go of the rage, the anger, the poison of hatred that enslaves us to those who have caused our pain, and so providing ourselves a space for a healthier view of life.

When I was finally ready to let go of my anger and hurt, I spent a great deal of time crying out to God. Being ready to let go and being free of anger don't happen at the same time. I read a lot of the psalms. At that time one of my favorites was Psalm 94. "God of vengeance, Yahweh, God of vengeance, shine forth! Arise, judge of the world, give back the proud what they deserve! How long are the wicked, Yahweh, how long are the wicked to triumph?" Here I was crying out to the God of vengeance, begging Him to give the wicked what they deserve: annihilation! There is something freeing about giving anger to God. Letting it go, but not just into thin air. Giving those angry feelings that were no longer sustaining me over to God, my refuge, freed me to breathe again. But I didn't laugh right away. The laughter didn't begin until six months later when the surgeon successfully reversed my colostomy and reconnected my bowel so that I was put back together again, almost as good as new.

Ahh, but the story is not over. Remember the minor surgery that had led to the perforated bowel? The cyst that needed to be removed? Well, it seems there never *was* a cyst. It was scar tissue masquerading as a cyst. I hadn't needed surgery after all.

I have been asked by many people, especially the nurses who hear the story of my colostomy, why I was no longer angry? I don't know with certainty. Somewhere along the way, I accepted that life happens, and not always in the way we hope. I cannot control events. I choose not to ask myself why bad things happen to good people and good things happen to bad people. I choose not to fall into the abyss of theodicy. Ultimately, it doesn't matter why we suffer. What truly affects our quality of life is how we react. It is only how we react that is in our hands, and an ethic of rights and responsibilities demands of us that we choose. The Judeo-Christian ethic pushes us to choose to let anger and revenge go, because leaving it unchecked will lead us into victimhood and violence. So I believe I am not bitter or angry because sometime during my life I made a conscious choice not to be.

The words *victim* and *survivor* are used a lot today. They're labels. I don't like labels. I choose to be neither victim nor survivor. I am a compilation of all my past experiences: physical, mental, emotional, and spiritual. They are the chapters in the Book of Me. To live your best life, you accept the person you have become as a result of all your life experiences. I am an open book with many chapters yet to be written.

I recently read a commentary on the book Ecclesiastes that changed my understanding of its message; this commentary speaks to my choices in life. I had always pictured the author of Ecclesiastes, "the Preacher," as an elderly man with unruly grey hair, sitting on his high back chair, cane in hand, pontificating on the futility and unfairness of life. I was left with a sense of sadness when I finished the book, because the Preacher seemed so bitter. And based on other explanations I have read, I thought this was the only way to read the book. But this interpretation gave me a whole new perspective. The commentator wrote, "The sad but gentle Preacher brings this advice to us: The enjoyment of life is itself God's gift. Let us therefore enjoy every minute of life. We must know that for everything there is a proper time. Take advantage of youth, while we have it. And, above all, reverence God and keep His commandments." We must also come to know that life is God's own gift to us, that we should remember that the days of our lives are few and that God approves of us being happy.[165] The commentator takes most of this interpretation from verses 5:17–19:

> So my conclusion is this: true happiness lies in eating and drinking and enjoying whatever has been achieved under the sun, throughout the life given by God: for this is the lot of humanity. And whenever God gives someone riches and property, with the ability to enjoy them and find contentment in work, this is a gift from God. For such a person will hardly notice the passing of time, so long as God keeps his heart occupied with joy.

Different writers have different perspectives. The different commentators on Ecclesiastes had read the same book but had come away with totally different feelings. One chose to focus on futility and one on joy. Bitter or better. And I think this perspective has been mine, subconsciously, most of my life; this made it possible for me to laugh in my distress and choose life rather than victimhood, which for me is a type of death.

After my surgeries, a strange thing happened. Before my ordeal, all I had wanted to do in life was to consume the written word.

Now here I was, freed from all schedules. I had absolute freedom to read whenever I wanted, as long as I wanted, undisturbed. Funny thing: I now discovered that I could not focus on the written word. I couldn't put a thought into a sentence. I had anxiety attacks in bookstores and I couldn't enter a library. Before, I had always loved walking along the aisles of libraries and bookstores, even when I wasn't looking for a particular book. I would let my fingers flutter languidly over the spines of the books as I passed by until one would catch my attention. That pleasure was now gone; now I could find comfort only at the racks of magazines.

I was drawn to those magazines that were devoted to decorating and filled with photographs. Me, a woman who hated shopping, even for groceries. I admit I had a rather snobby attitude toward Martha Stewart and her followers. How could anyone spend their days hovering over magazines that showed you how to dress a kitchen in the latest style? And now there I was, doing exactly that. I suppose it was a compromise of sorts. If I couldn't focus on what was written in a newspaper or a good book, I could at least turn the slick pages of style magazines and enjoy the pictures. Then I became a devotee. I devoured all kinds of decorating magazines and even watched the latest home decorating shows on TV. I would get a thrill when I would return from the mailbox with my most recent magazine tucked under my arm! And I started to collect books on gardening. I had been introduced to gardening at my father's knee, but had had little pleasure in it for a very long time. But here I was, collecting books about whimsical gardens.

I had always craved books. I had so loved reading and libraries as a young girl that I turned my room into a pretend lending library. Now I looked at my book collection and dusted it, while exploring all things creative. I had lost the ability to write as well as to understand most of what I was reading. I had just finished my university degree and my hospital chaplaincy residency, which required reading and writing and synthesizing ideas across disciplines, but now recalling the word for even a simple thing, like "lamp," was painful.

I have heard that some people react very badly to general anesthetic; it impairs their ability to focus and understand. I also was dealing with depression that had taken hold of me a year earlier. Compound that depression with the depression from my ordeal with the surgeries, and my brain was just cotton candy. My memory had been shattered into a million shards, each carrying a small piece from my mind; a word here, a thought there.

I remember trying to write a eulogy for my mother when she died in 2008. I knew what I wanted to say. I tried to write it down. But nothing flowed. The sentences didn't follow each other properly. I had trouble finding words that had once been so familiar but now were gone. My daughter, who had come home for the funeral, sat down with what I had written and had to rewrite it.

Over the years I have read the stories of many others. There is comfort in knowing you are not alone. Kay Redfield Jamison, Professor of Psychiatry at Johns Hopkins School of Medicine when she wrote *An Unquiet Mind* in 1994, noted that, "Reading, which had been at the heart of my intellectual and emotional existence, was suddenly beyond my grasp. I was used to reading three or four books a week; now it was impossible. I did not read a serious work of literature [or] nonfiction cover to cover, for more than ten years."

Ten years on, and I am again reading and writing. Slowly the pieces of memory are reconnecting, although many seem to be held together with gauze. I still have reminders of the surgeries and the depressions. I would be lying if I didn't say that there are times that are still very dark. I had to learn to let go of my depression. As odd as that sounds, mental illness has been my companion for a long time, and over time I became attached to the dark side of my life. It is a place I know well. I was afraid to let go of that part of me that was half of my personality.

Depression can actually be a wellspring of creativity. It was in the dark places that I found my voice. It was there that I most felt pain of others. It was there that my righteous anger welled up, demanding that I respond to the injustices that I saw around me. What if I let go of that darkness, I wondered? What if I stopped my falls into the abyss? Would I still "feel"? Would I still be able to write? Wellness sometimes demands of us that we let go, but fear holds us back. Amputating a part of your behavior can be as frightening as amputating a limb. I had to learn that letting go of the part of me that was defined by depression would not lead to the melting away of the "me" that I knew. I was able to let go of my depression and no longer had the desire or the need to go back into the darkness.

Every once in a while, though, when the darkness comes to call, I do welcome it. I like to embrace it for a short while. A friend who also dealt with severe depression sent me this eloquent description of living with depression. It was written in 1904 by German poet Rainer Maria Rilke in *Letters to a Young Poet*, and is titled "The Work Being Accomplished Within You."

> *So don't be frightened, dear friend, if a sadness confronts you larger than any you have ever known, casting its shadow over all you do. You must think that something is happening within you, and remember that life has not forgotten you; it holds you in its hand and will not let you fall. Why would you want to exclude from your life any uneasiness, any pain, any depression, since you don't know what work they are accomplishing within you?*

With experience comes wisdom—if we are open to it. I have learned that the darkness will lift. I know the pain will pass—usually with medication. Although I am not angry, I have moments when I do go traipsing down memory lane, gently touching some of those familiar angry memories that kept me alive so many years ago. But I won't stay too long. I know that anger is not my friend.

> *And God cried, His tears falling to His altar.*
> *And the Holy Spirit fled to the Wailing Wall to mourn.*
> *My soul shattered into a million pieces,*
> *like the sparks of the cosmos.*
> *And I searched for me,*
> *and I looked for God.*
> *Like Jacob on his ladder, I too wrestled and was wounded.*
> *And just as Jacob became Israel, I too will be reborn.*
> *I will find myself and my place in time and space*
> *when I find God.*
> *For God, the divine spark, is in me.*

When was the last time you thanked God for your health, for the ability to stand before Him? I'm guessing not as often as you have thanked your car mechanic. I believe that religion is the gift that enables us to face the suffering and tragedy that crosses the path of each and every one of us at some point in our lives. For me, the picture or thought of God caring for me, always beside me, holding on to me, gave me a sense of protection and space in which to cope each day with whatever came to pass; and on many of those days, pain came by to visit.

I am sure that others have different pictures to focus on, but for me, God holds a connection to the past as well as the present. This is the God to whom my parents, Abraham and Sarah, my grandparents, and all my ancestors, all the way back to the first Abraham and Sarah, prayed. We are connected, past and present, through this God. "No one person is alone when he can cling to a chain of tradition in which he is the latest link."[166]

When our ancestors first stepped forth out of the cave to explore and to hunt, they faced many frightening moments. Would the hunter be the predator—or the prey? We know from neuroscience that our ancestor would have an immediate physiological response: his heart rate would go up; his breathing would become more labored; his intestines would clench; hormones would be shooting through his body and adrenalin would be flowing. His body would be preparing for fight or flight. He was physically prepared for battle: a battle for his life and food for his family.

Now, imagine his feelings after that encounter. He is alive. His body responds by normalizing his breath and blood pressure; his intestines relax; the adrenalin must be reabsorbed; and his legs are probably shaking, perhaps to the point that he collapses, like a marathon runner at the end of a 26-mile run. He is on his knees. His head is probably bent because it feels like it weighs a ton, so he holds it in his hands.

And now he can think; about what happened and about what could have happened. And then he releases a sigh of relief, what

---

166 Rabbi Lookstein, source unknown.

Edward Sapir in *Language: An Introduction to the Study of Speech* calls an involuntary utterance, an indication of an overflow of emotion, an instinctive cry that is universal.[167]

This primal cry has a name. It is the cry of gratitude. Any time that he thinks about that experience, he will relive the emotion; he will experience fear and then fall on his knees in gratitude to his Creator as if it had happened just moments ago. And he will pass this primal instinct of gratitude to his descendants: a genetic memory.

There are families who find themselves physically separated for periods of time but who still have a need to be together, emotionally or spiritually. Imagine a father whose work demands that he travel a great deal and a child who misses him. The father tries to comfort the son before he leaves on his next trip. *Look up at the moon tonight, my son,* he says, and *I will be looking at the moon, too.* Although they are miles apart, they will take comfort in that shared experience.

---

[167] Edward Sapir, *Language: An Introduction to the Study of Speech* (New York: Harcourt Brace, 1921), http://www.bartleby.com/186/1.html.

XXIII
"MY GOD, MY GOD, WHY HAVE YOU FORSAKEN ME?"

Prayer cannot mend a broken bridge, rebuild a ruined city or bring water to parched fields. Prayer can mend a broken heart, lift up a discouraged soul and strengthen a weakened soul.

—Ferdinand M. Isserman

One of my patients was a young mother of two small children. She had just received a diagnosis of breast cancer, and I was called to her room. Her husband and children were in the room with her, completely distraught. I pulled a chair up to her bedside. And listened. "Why me?" she asked. "I'm a good mother. I take care of my children. Why me, and not the woman down the street? She's never home with her kids. Why me?"

Stories like this make me think. How often have you said aloud after something extraordinarily wonderful happened to you, "Why, God? Why me? Why did you choose me, to anoint my head with oil, so much so that my cup runneth over?" We accept blessings as part of the everyday course of living, but we question sadness and pain because we assume that we deserve better. "A moment's adversity and pleasures are forgotten" (Ecclesiasticus 11:27). We are turning into a nation of people who are consumed with grandiose, infantile delusions of entitlement.

Do we deserve good things? Do we earn them? If we do all the "right things," why are we not rewarded? Perhaps the fault resides in the initial assumption that doing all the right things will lead to great blessings. Maimonides, a great Jewish philosopher, talked about the many levels of loving God. Some people love and honor God in expectation of a reward. Some love and honor God in hopes of balancing the books: three kindnesses here to balance the lack of compassion there. At the highest level, we love and honor God simply because He exists. Not for some reward. Not to avoid punishment. And the same needs to hold true for people we love. Do we love them for what they do for us? Do we deny that love when we are hurt by them? Or do we love them because they are?

Some people believe that if they are kind and just, bad things in life will be mitigated. The story of Job is in the Biblical canon to make us question all of these assumptions. Job, the enigmatic metaphor of suffering, lived believing that he had always behaved in a way that honored God. Satan suggested to God that it is easy to honor God when life is good, and Job's life was good. But what would happen if Job faced great challenges, painful challenges? And so the test began; the first reality show. Everything that mattered to Job, everything that makes life worth living, was taken away; and what mattered most was family and health. Friends urged him to admit that he had done something wrong and beg God's forgiveness. But Job was steadfast. Then he finally confronts God, asking Him why these things had happened to him, a man who devoted his life to honoring Him. The question is heartbreaking. It is a question that torments so many of us.

God's answer is enigmatic.

> Brace yourself like a fighter: I am going to ask the questions, and you are to inform me! Where were you when I laid down the earth's foundations? Tell me since you are so well-informed! Who decided its dimensions, do you know? Or who stretched the measuring line across it? Who supports its pillars at the base? Job 38:3–6

God tells Job that he was not present at the beginning of creation and will not be there at the end. And we are left to ask, what does that mean? After almost forty chapters dealing with suffering, we are left with a feeling of anxiety because we have not been given a definitive answer about suffering and evil, and living with ambiguity can be unbearable to us. So we search for absolute answers to assuage the unbearableness.

Some people believe that everything is God's will. Unfortunately, they will always be victims of circumstance, because they believe they have no control and life "just happens" to them. Others believe that they can affect God's will by following a particular dogma. If they do what they are told by their preachers, all will be well. Unfortunately, when life does not go well, their suffering intensifies because they take on the guilt of failure. Then there are those who do not believe that God exists and we are on our own. The story of Job is timeless because it opens the door to deep, internal soul-searching that each of us needs to do during our lifetimes: because life is not simple, while our yearning for meaning is multilayered.

That yearning reaches its pinnacle when tragedy strikes. Did Adam and Eve remain steadfast in their love for their son Cain after he killed Abel? The Bible doesn't say much about how they felt or how they dealt with the death of their son. How does a parent deal with the death of a child? And not just a death—a murder. And the murder was committed by the brother! Did Adam and Eve have unconditional love for Cain? Did they recover from the death of their beloved son at the hand of the other beloved son? Did they find closure? We want answers. We have trouble accepting that life is difficult. It has been since Adam and Eve left the Garden.

We struggle with coming to terms with all the "what ifs." Then we hear about healing and closure. What do these words mean? Are we expected to simply accept whatever has happened? How does one accept tragedy? Nietzsche said, "That which does not kill us makes us stronger." I met someone who said that if it doesn't kill you, it can make you weaker. It's true. It can make you weaker, but you make that choice.

We can choose how we will respond to any and all events because our thought circuitry, our emotional circuitry, and our physiological circuitry are all connected to our multidimensional behavioral circuitry.[168] Free will not only allows us to choose life, it demands it of us: "Today, I call heaven and earth to witness against

---

[168] Taylor, *Insight*, 163.

you: I am offering you life or death, blessing or curse. Choose life, then, so that you and your descendants may live" (Deuteronomy 30:19–20).

We choose to live for those who came before us so that we can keep alive their knowledge and wisdom. We live for our children and our children's children so that we can transmit to them all that we have learned. We live and continue to live in the hope that we will find new meaning and purpose in our life. We live and continue to live because of our obligation to honor God: "The dead cannot praise Yahweh, those who sink into silence, but we, the living, shall bless Yahweh, henceforth and forever" (Psalm 115:17).

In *Messengers of God*, Elie Wiesel, a Holocaust survivor, takes us on a journey through the trials and tribulations of Job. Wiesel is angry with the ending of the story: Job's immediate surrender to God after God rebuked him. Why did Job not demand an answer from God for all the pain and suffering? What of justice for his children, taken from this life through no fault of their own? And yet, Job agreed to live, again. As Wiesel points out: "Therein lies God's true victory: He forced Job to welcome happiness. After the catastrophe, Job lived happily in spite of himself."[169]

> *Therein lies God's true victory: He forced Job to welcome happiness. After the catastrophe, Job lived happily in spite of himself.*
>
> —Elie Wiesel

When we are physically wounded, scar tissue will eventually form over the wound. At first, the new skin is very thin, weak, and vulnerable. If the wound is not cared for properly, it can reopen, forcing the healing process to begin all over again. But over time, a physical wound that is cared for will heal and the scar tissue that covers it can be stronger than the original layer of skin. So, too, with the heart and the soul. The initial wound can be so deep as to almost kill, not the physical body, but the soul. But like skin tissue, the soul, too can heal. Over time the scar over the wounded soul

---

[169] Wiesel, *Messengers*, 234.

will become stronger, perhaps even stronger than the original covering.

Freud wrote that religion is a crutch and not something a mature adult should need. Yet when one breaks one's leg, a crutch is necessary for healing. Once the bone is repaired, the crutch is put away—for another day. So when a soul is wounded, why should the need for a crutch be childish? Religion can be that crutch, the reminder that one is not alone, that God is playing a part in the journey, step by step. He carries us, sheltering us with His Presence.

Our need for closeness to God changes. There are times in our lives when God just flutters at the edges of our awareness. And then there are the times when we reach out to God to keep us from falling off a cliff. At these moments prayer, ritual, traditions, and community become part of the healing of the soul just as a cast plays a role in the healing of a broken bone.

Some people go through life without any apparent need for God or for communal symbols, rituals, or traditions, and they suggest to others that we each must make our own way through life's passages. I listened to a woman on the radio recalling the suffering she experienced with the death of a much-beloved husband. She preached that mourning was personal, not communal. Each mourner needs to find her own path through the pain. Do what feels good, she said. Lie in bed all day. Don't get dressed if you don't feel up to it. It isn't necessary to send thank-you notes to acknowledge those who have sent cards, letters, flowers, or donations in the name of the loved one.

Yet writing notes of thanks gives the mourner an opportunity to find reasons to be grateful at the darkest time. Each note written reminds the mourner that she is loved by others. Each time she puts pen to paper, she will remember some special moment that she and her husband shared with that particular member of the family or that particular friend.

We live in a society that expends enormous amounts of energy sharing every moment of life via tweets, Facebook, and all manner of social media, yet death is to be made into a private matter? Death is not a private matter. Just as God was present to bless Isaac after the death of his father, Abraham, and bury His beloved Moses, in our desire to imitate God, we, too, need to honor the dead and comfort the mourner, because each death is a loss of light to the Lord. Death is no more a private matter than birth. We come into the world to family and community surrounding us with love. Family and community are also there for us in death. "Fear not death; we are destined to die. We share it with all who ever lived, with all who ever be."[170]

Religion provides the mourners and the community with rituals, tradition, and symbols to honor the one who has died, to give voice to those who remain behind and provide them a way back to the living. St. Augustine described the Christian sacraments as an outward and visible sign of an inward invisible state.[171]

My child, shed tears over the dead,
Lament for the dead to show your sorrow,
then bury the body with due ceremony
and do not fail to honor the grave.
Weep bitterly, beat your breast,
Observe the mourning the dead deserves . . .
And then be comforted in your sorrow;
For grief can lead to death,
A grief-stricken heart loses all energy . . .
Once the dead are laid to rest, let their memory rest,
Do not fret for them, once their spirit departs.

Ecclesiasticus 38:16

We follow ritual and tradition for the same reason we follow a map: to get from one place to another without losing our way. My parents died fourteen years apart. I had already traveled with friends and family as they had walked the path of grief. I participated in the rituals and traditions of death, burial, and mourning with them. Accompanying others becomes a dress rehearsal for the day when we must face the death of a loved one, when we must say good-bye to a friend, a spouse, a parent, and the most painful of all, a child.

---

[170] Adapted from Ben Sira, *Ecclesiasticus*, http://chevraed.org/benSira.html.
[171] Drew Gilpin Faust, *This Republic of Suffering*, 149.

When it was my turn to grieve the death of my parents, and with the death of my mother, my last parent, to accept becoming an orphan, I wasn't completely bereft or lost wandering in the desert with no landmarks to point the way, because the rituals and traditions were familiar to me and comforted me. Say this prayer; stand over here; move over there; shovel the dirt over the casket to confirm that death is real. I walked along the path with my friends and family walking with me, holding me upright.

Following a burial, many mourners practice the tradition of a communal meal. Food nourishes the body while the community, in sharing in the emotional pain, nourishes the soul. Religion provides a path that has been followed for centuries, a road that takes us from shock and numbness, loneliness and loss, to emotional and spiritual healing. We light candles. We sit together. We talk. We eat and drink together. We share memories of the one who has died and we cry, together. We learn to believe that we will once again find meaning in life. We behave as if it were true and with time we once again feel that we belong with the living. "You have turned my mourning into dancing, you have stripped off my sackcloth and clothed me with joy" (Psalm 30:11). Death will not defeat us.

My supervisor in chaplaincy, Ken Jackson, shared with us a story about one of his parishioners whose wife had died. Ken dropped by the house a few days after her death. The widower was consumed by the death of his wife and was not coping at all. So Ken asked him for a cup of tea. The widower found his way around the kitchen, put water in the kettle and set it on the flame, and found a tea bag and put it into the cup. Then Ken asked for some milk and sugar to go with it. Ken wasn't thirsty. He actually wasn't fond of tea. But the rituals involved in making tea forced this man to affirm life while confronting death. Mourning rituals, symbols, and traditions envelop those who suffer, keeping them in this world while helping them to accept that someone they love is no longer with us and that they, the living, are part of a sacred chain.

Our Father Who art in heaven,
All merciful and full of compassion,
Healer of the broken-hearted, hallowed be
Thy name.

Unfortunately, in our day we have been led to expect total emotional "closure" following a catastrophic event, from the death of a loved one to the death of a dream. I have lost track of the number of books, articles, television programs, and gurus who have told us how to grieve and find closure. It is an industry. We want answers when life falls off the rails, when it veers from our carefully, lovingly planned path. Rare are those amongst us who choose chaos over control. When we lose control, we turn to anyone who says, "I have the answer. Come, follow me." And we do. We take their plan, from their personal experience, as if there were a one-size-fits-all pattern for grieving. So we follow their way . . . and yet we gain no closure.

Speaking as a professional chaplain, I believe it is facile, disingenuous, and mean-spirited for counselors to promote the concept of total closure. It is my experience that seeking closure is an exercise in futility. Human beings are not obligated to accept a tragedy. Rather, to survive, we must come to terms with it by accepting and embracing the person we *become* because of the tragedy. And that requires forgiveness, especially of ourselves. First, we must forgive ourselves for our anger and hurt. We must forgive ourselves our guilt and our sense of failure. We ask God to forgive us our trespasses. And from His forgiveness we learn that we can forgive others. We forgive, not for their sake, but for our own. For those we cannot forgive, for events that are evil, we leave forgiveness to God. As long as we carry anger or hate towards another, we are in a damaging relationship with that person.

Life is a not a book of separate, neat, distinct chapters, as if the past experience can be put behind us, behind a door. It takes time and work to let things go. Forgiveness that comes too soon, too quickly, is superficial. But too often, others will tell us this isn't so. "It is done," they will tell us. "Put it away. End of chapter. Now, move on, carry on, look to the future." How unfair to the heart and the soul. The chapters and verses of life are interconnected, sometimes flowing one into the other, but other times so disjointed that looking back one wonders, "Whose life was this?" Life ebbs and flows with times of joy and sorrow and with intermittent, quiet, restful times that each soul needs to recuperate, to adjust to the loss—waiting for the right time to begin again, to dream again, to look outward with hope and renewal.

With the death of a spouse or a relationship, we have to develop a new story and learn a new dance, without our loved one. With the loss of the familiar, the known, the expected, we feel awkward and out of step and frustrated and lost, and this can make us fearful and unsure of ourselves. Then, just as we become accustomed to our new solitary dance, we find ourselves blessed with a new partner; a new opportunity for love and affection; someone with whom we can lay down new memories and shared experiences. You would expect this transition into something new to be so much easier than facing and accepting loss. But it isn't. Oddly enough, this blessing is accompanied with tears—some of joy, but also many of sorrow.

We look forward with hope, while at the same time memories come cascading down around us, some good, some painful. Almost against our will, we find ourselves looking backward to what was and all that was lost. For a moment, we are caught like Lot's wife, who turned to salt when she looked back as she walked away from her home. Like her, we are caught between past and future. We know we are moving forward to a new beginning, a new life, but we feel held back, even if only for the briefest of moments, to say one last goodbye to the past. And in that moment we are like the pillar of salt, preserved in time between what was and what could be.

Eric Kandel, a psychiatrist, neuroscientist, and Nobel Prize winner, says that human memory reinvents itself all the time. Every time we remember something, our mind changes it a little bit. The memory becomes a mixture of past events, past images, pictures, words, facts and fiction. Kandel calls it "re:collection."[172] Dr. Lionel Tiger has conducted research that suggests that the brain gives imagined events the same value and authority as what we tangibly experience. Our brain gives us the gift of personal storytelling.[173]

Using our imagination, we can revisit the past. We can look back and embrace the memories that raise us up, lighten our burden, and

---

[172] Erick Kandel, "Speaking Memory," *Scientific American Mind*, Oct. 2008.
[173] Charles Lewis, "God's Brain: The Neuroscience of Devotion," *National Post*, March 13, 2010, http:// life.nationalpost.com/ 2010/03/13/ gods-brain-the-neuroscience-of-devotion/.

envelop us with love. We can acknowledge anxiety, depression, anger, and hurt in our lives and make a conscious decision to change. We can envision the person we want to be and move towards that ideal. We can choose to repent, to forgive, to accept, to love. We can choose to embrace our imperfections and frailties, but we must at least accept our imperfections so we can truly believe that we are still lovable and loved—in spite of our frailties. Then we can embrace the imperfections of others, especially those we love. Our feelings towards the past, present, and future are critical for the development of our soul and its relationship to God and the universe.

XXIV
Finding Grace at the Table

Praise the person who keeps a splendid table.
Ecclesiasticus 31:28

Eat what is offered you like a well brought-up person.
Ecclesiasticus 31:16

Religious rituals, traditions, and symbols connect us to the sacred. Whenever I have chicken soup, I remember Fridays when I was growing up. The morning always began with my mother and my grandmother preparing food in the kitchen. There were no prepared foods to pick up because everything was homemade and made from scratch, except for the bread, which was special for the Sabbath. My grandmother was all of five feet tall—on a good day. She stood erect like a stoic wood soldier, though. Her hair was wavy steel grey that gently curled under at her chin. She always had the same facial expression: stern. She never changed. She always looked old to me. She would stand over the stove, frying the onions, getting the potatoes ready to fill with ground beef. And she added extra salt to the soup. By dinnertime, the house was filled with the rich and savory aromas of chicken soup, roast beef or chicken, potatoes, and some kind of freshly baked pie. My mother had a talent for making the best pies.

So Friday was always special, but when we had company, the table was exemplary. White linens and cloth napkins—paper were an *everyday* item, not good enough for Friday night. In those days, my mother did the laundry in a wringer washer. The tub swished the laundry but there was no spin cycle. The laundry was taken out by hand and put through the wringer: two rollers through which the laundry *was pulled* by turning a crank. Then she would take the wet clothes up the stairs and outside on the porch and hang them up on the line. In wet weather or really cold weather, the clothes were left to dry on a line in the basement. No going to the dry cleaner. The tablecloths and napkins were ironed at home.

My mother put out the "good dishes" and the company cutlery and the best glasses. No bottles were allowed on the table. Condiments were put in little bowls. I remember my mother lighting the Sabbath candles with my grandmother beside her. They would bow their heads, place their hands before their eyes, and quietly invoke the prayer over light. My father would stand proudly at the head of the table, lift his cup of wine in one hand and the prayer book in the other, and with joy he would pronounce the blessing over the wine and then say the Friday night prayer. He would say the blessing over the bread for the Sabbath, cut it, salt it, and pass it around. On some Friday nights my out-of-town cousins would join us. And other times, strangers were sitting at the table; they were always new to Canada. My father would attempt to explain some kind of familial relationship, not that it ever really mattered. They were starting a new life. We were helping them. It was at this table that I learned the meaning of good deeds, kindness to others, and charity. It wasn't discussed. It was learned by experience.

Ritual makes the ephemeral concrete. It makes what we cannot see tangible. Ritual is to religion what poetry is to language. It adds extra layers of meaning to the mundane of the everyday. Ritual connects us one to the other and to community in a special time, free from the distractions of everyday madness, of instant communication and constant interruption. By handing down a ritual we are bringing the past into the present, preparing to hand it down to those who come after. We bring the memories of those who have gone before us into our presence.

Ritual combines nostalgia, memories of the past, and spirituality; it creates a connection beyond us, into one space and one place, one moment in time. There is a Hebrew blessing that brings past and present together with the promise of the season that will follow. It is called the *Shekhiyanu*:

> *Blessed are You, Lord, our God,*
> *King of the universe,*

Who has kept us alive, sustained us,
and enabled us to reach this season.

We are losing our connection to ritual, though. Life is running at a faster pace than ever before. Computers have not made life easier. Instant communication makes great demands on us. We are expected to be on call all the time. We no longer have to do the laundry by hand or in a wringer washer and then take it out to dry. Ironing has become a thing of the past, with no-iron materials and the dry cleaner. Most meals can be purchased or catered. We now have so many ways to save time and yet so few of us take, or make, the time to eat together. We are losing a sense of the sacred—the sacredness of family, friends, community. We are forgetting that life is in the details.

When the Israelites escaped from their enslavement in Egypt and began their forty-year sojourn in the desert, they were told by God to build a table of gold to be set inside the Tent of Meeting, God's sanctuary. All the dishes, cups, jars, and bowls were to be made of gold as well. And twelve loaves of bread were to be placed on the table, in two rows of six, on each Sabbath. The table became a sacred place for sacred time together. Today, in our haste to move on to the next activity, we have forgotten the importance of grace at the sacred table. When you rush through the day, grab the children from soccer or hockey or ballet and drive through the local take-out, do you even have a moment to think about the food you are about to eat, or the work that has gone into making that food available? Or is eating just another bodily function that has to be taken care of before the next event? When was the last time you drove through the take-out window and said grace? When was the last time you said grace?

It is time again to make a point of taking the time to sit down, look at, and appreciate food. Think about the convergence of nature and nurture, God and humankind coming together to provide this sustenance. That piece of bread did not miraculously arrive at the table the way manna was delivered to the Israelites by God in the desert. Think about the work that went into making that piece of bread: the soil, the rain, the sun, the seed, the care, the growing, the harvesting, the baking, and the delivery to you. And be grateful.

Gratitude forces us to take the time to savor the flavor of food. Paying attention to our food, chewing it slowly, as our parents taught us, feeling the texture, thinking about the flavors just as one mulls the undercurrents of a good wine, helps us to reconnect to those who produce the food, to the earth from which it came, and to God. It is no wonder we are told to *concentrate* on our meals—rather than viewing food as merely a nourishing accompaniment to watching television, reading, or texting.

Eating can be a spiritual activity. It brings us together in community, be it family or friends. It is a place to develop and build on tradition, ritual, and symbols that tie people and families together. Planning for a gathering takes on special meaning. How many of us have spent a great deal of time setting the table just so, debating over every detail? Think of the number of magazines and articles and television shows that teach the pleasures of the table. We are, in a sense, preparing a sacred place for a sacred time together. Does it not make sense to spend but a moment being grateful for that place and time?

This is spirituality: connecting the everyday to something even greater, the mundane to the sacred. No matter how grand or meager the meal, being together, savoring the time and the flavors, brings out in us gratitude that soothes the heart and soul. If we come to the table conscious of the moment, acknowledging the work, the care and the love, the table will be a sacred place for all.

> *This is spirituality: connecting the everyday to something even greater, the mundane to the sacred.*

I remember sitting down to lunch some years ago in a beautiful restaurant in Chicago. Sitting at a table near us were about a dozen people. Suddenly, they rose and began to sing a Gregorian chant before they ate. Gregorian chant is hauntingly beautiful music. It is claimed by some that it is the last remnant of the music the Levites sang in the Temple in Jerusalem. That day in the restaurant, one could not help but be taken with the music and the mystery of the moment, to join these people in their joy, their gratitude, their belief, whether one believed in God or not. The moment was electric for all in the restaurant. For a moment, all of us came together. For some, the music might have triggered a sense of nostalgia for family or tradition, or what could have been, if only . . .

Saying grace over a meal is more than an act of gratitude. It is a doorway to the past, the present, and the future, tugging at our memory, tugging at our yearning for a greater connection than the moment itself.

Manna was given to the Israelites in the desert. It was given to them by God. It was a concrete sign of God's presence. That God will nourish the body and the soul. Just as manna had a different taste to each person, God is internalized differently by each of us. We take what we need as God gave as needed. Food for the body and the soul has come together from the beginning of God's revelation to the Israelites. It is felt and tasted, seen and inhaled, both literally and metaphorically, because the more senses that are involved in learning, the better the lesson is learned. And Jesus gave to the apostles in the Eucharist both bread and wine, the body and the blood: when someone partakes, they are seeing, tasting, feeling, inhaling, as well as listening to the word, so that it becomes part of both their body and their soul. One is entwined in the other.

XXV
YOU SHALL HAVE
NO OTHER GODS TO RIVAL ME

The sun was high in the sky, and it was growing warmer. All will be well; God sees to it that the harmony may not be destroyed, all will be well; history moves on, and men, after all, weren't created just to slaughter one another.

—Elie Wiesel[174]

There are some people who claim that Eastern religions and philosophies are more "authentic" than monotheism because these religions have no single authority, no Divine God, who makes demands on individual and community behavior.

Chuang-Tzu, a Taoist philosopher, saw human life as a dream from which one need not awaken. There is no self and no awakening from the dream of self, he taught.[175] Taoism also does not believe in tying one to a single set of morals, rules, or principles. The good life has no particular purpose, according to Chuang-Tzu, one merely responds to events: "I enter with the inflow, and emerge with the outflow, follow the Way of the water, and do not impose my selfishness upon it. This is how I stay afloat."[176] The Taoist goes with the flow, while following a path that seeks harmony, peace, and longevity. Taoism looks to the animal kingdom as a paradigm for living well. Animals do not need to think or choose. There is no concept of the ideal way to live, no "ought" versus "is." One does what feels right at the time. There is no intentionality. No thought of consequences. No sense of anxiety regarding decision-making. In Taoism, the good life "means living

---

174 Wiesel, *The Gates of the Forest*, 49.
175 Gray, Straw Dogs, 81.
176 Ibid.

effortlessly, according to our nature. The freest human being is not one who acts on reasons he has chosen for himself, but one who never has to choose. Rather than agonizing over alternatives, he responds effortlessly to situations as they arrive."[177]

The Taoist prioritizes the right side of the brain, the side that lives in the moment.

Buddhism, one of the better known of the Eastern philosophies, is based instead on the individual finding his own true, authentic self. This is done through the established teachings of the Four Noble Truths that explain the cause and cessation of suffering, and the Eightfold Path that explains the way to end suffering.

Buddhism's roots in human history are deep. It began in India 2500 years ago and flourishes today throughout the modern world. In North America there are five Buddhist traditions: Pure Land, Nicheren, Theravada, Tibetan Mahayana, and Zen. The fundamental assumption in Buddhism is that suffering is caused by the human desire for acquisitions: people or things. To lose the desire requires losing the sense of the "I", the ego, the self, the home of desire. Releasing oneself from desire is a long and difficult process that cannot be completed in one lifetime. Buddhists believe that one returns to earth many times, through cycles of reincarnation, until one finally achieves *nirvana*, which is defined as the cessation of suffering.

Buddhists practice meditation as a means to reduce desire. The purpose of this meditation is mindfulness. Today we think of mindfulness as "paying close attention to what we are doing in the moment," what some call "being present" or "grounding oneself" and concentrating on and enjoying the moment. But mindfulness in Buddhism is much deeper and more profound; it requires concentrating on each aspect of the body, from breathing to feelings.

The purpose of mindful breathing is to calm the body by depersonalizing the breathing process until one loses all sense of the self. Mindfulness with regard to feelings requires that one pay

---

[177] Ibid., 114–5.

attention to the feeling (for example, anger), until the feeling disperses, rather than paying attention to the person or thing toward which the anger is aimed. To practice enhanced mindfulness requires a type of concentration that will tranquilize the mind and lead to an altered state of consciousness, a total absorption or focus where the mind is totally occupied with shutting down all other senses.[178] Ultimately, one is seeking a state of internal peace by dispersing the emotions that lead to a state of desire, and therefore to suffering.

When we human beings were sent out from the Garden of Eden to find our authentic selves, we were not instructed to do it by meditating our way there. Nor were we ever instructed to hide from our emotions. God, in creating us, gave us every emotion, including pain and sorrow, loss and suffering. And our emotions are like naturally occurring events, which are neither good nor bad. It is our response to our feelings and natural disasters that define us.

The prophet Jeremiah denounced as false prophets those who retreated into denial. The Athenians believed that one could only achieve liberation by going through sorrow, not by going to "elaborate lengths to make sure that it never impinged on your protected existence."[179] As Allen Francis, Professor Emeritus and former Chairman of Psychiatry at Duke University wrote, grief and sorrow are "the necessary price we all pay for having the ability to love other people. Our lives consist of a series of attachment and inevitable losses and evolution has given us the emotional tools to handle both."[180]

Think of the Bible as a story of the evolution of behavior, emotion, and thought. Think of God as the role model. At first, He appears to be vengeful and vindictive. Over time, though, He seems to change and become just and merciful, charitable and full of loving kindness. But "no; I, Yahweh, do not change" (Malachi 3:6). God does not evolve. God is perfect. God is. We learn from Him that our behavior, our emotions and thoughts evolve. We do that

---

[178] Ibid., 911–2.
[179] Karen Armstrong, *The Great Transformation*, 355.
[180] Allen Francis, "Good Grief," *New York Times*, August 14, 2010, http://www.nytimes.com/ 2010/08/15/ opinion/15frances.html.

by facing our feelings of anger and revenge so that we can come to a compassionate, just, and merciful emotional place. Rather than expend energy trying to remove thoughts of desire that could lead to suffering, the Bible, the Psalms, the Prophets, and the Wisdom Literature allow us to explore all our feelings.

Leaving the Garden required that we make use of all the emotions we were given, as a means of survival. Fear and aggression prevented our extinction. Energy was put into fighting for survival, discovering new ways of hunting, then gathering and planting and harvesting. Energy was spent on thinking and implementing ideas through action. Konrad Lorenz, an Austrian Nobel Prize winner and the founder of an area of science referred to as *ethology*, the scientific study of animal behavior, suggested that aggression is an innate behavior and if it were eliminated we "might destroy at the same time many of the highest forms of human achievement."[181] Aggressiveness pushes us to find new solutions to old problems, new products, new ways of thinking, and new discoveries that help us better understand ourselves and the world in which we live. And that mentality allowed Western culture and ethical monotheism to transform the world.

This is not to say that no discoveries have come from moments of quiet contemplation. But, I suggest, had we expended our energy by denying desire, repressing it, suppressing it, and overcoming a drive that is part of human nature from the inception of humankind, we would either be living just outside a cave with our children dying from disease, or we would be behaving like the Stepford Wives or Winnie-the-Pooh.[182] All of our emotions have significance.

Western culture developed along a different path from Eastern philosophies, a path not focused on internal transcendent peace or intuitive powers.[183] Faith in God was not meant to lead to self-denial. Faith is meant to elevate and improve man.[184] Our Hellenist philosophical ancestors "gravitated towards science and logos."[185]

---

[181] Leslie Stevenson, *Seven Theories of Human Nature*, 128.
[182] Benjamin Hoff, *The Tao of Pooh*.
[183] Armstrong, *Transformation*, 356.
[184] Wiesel, *Messengers*, 73.
[185] Armstrong, *Transformation*, 356.

Science and reason require imagination, inquisitiveness, a sense of wonder and awe, and a *desire* to explore and seek knowledge, new ideas, and new theories.

We dare to dream. We are pulled by the siren call of Pandora's Box. In the 1970s, George Steiner was writing about our loss of critical thinking, our moving away from the primacy of the left brain that is the seat of "the verbal, the Greek half, the ambitions, the dominating, the mastering half."[186] We have turned to other systems, including Eastern philosophies, for answers to our questions. These systems are contrary to Western culture. They promote "passivity against will; a theosophy of stasis and eternal return against a theodicy of historical progress; the focused monotony, even emptiness, of meditation and of meditative trance as opposed to logical, analytic reflection; asceticism against prodigality of person and expression; contemplation versus action."[187]

Being thrown out of the Garden, we had no choice but to become self-reliant, to create, to adapt and adjust, to exercise free will. But this came with obligations. We are to be as co-creators with God. When we were escorted out of the gates, it was not to be idle.

The Hebrew Bible and the Gospels admonish us to work: not simply to nurture what is before us, but to have dominion over all of creation, which requires management skills, husbandry, irrigation, cultivation, science, and respect for all of nature. During the Greco-Roman era, the philosophical teachings of Socrates, Plato, and Aristotle spread among the Jews of Palestine, including the idea that the "human soul has the divine gift of reason."[188]

There was a sharing of ideas and culture between the Greeks and the Jews. In the third century BCE, the Hebrew Bible was translated into Greek (the *Septuagint*), thus allowing the teachings of this ethical God to spread throughout the Greek world. The philosopher Philo, at the turn of the Common Era, synthesized

---

[186] Steiner, *Nostalgia*, 58.
[187] Steiner, *Nostalgia*, 45.
[188] Armstrong, *History*, 38.

Judaic teachings with Greek philosophy.[189] In the last third of the first century CE, Josephus the historian said, "Our earliest imitators were the Greek philosophers, who, through ostensibly observing the laws of their own countries, yet in their conduct and philosophy were Moses' disciples, holding similar views about God."[190]

When Rome conquered the Greeks, they incorporated many Greek beliefs into their own, and so the teachings spread. In the Holy Land, Jesus taught the word of God and, after his death, St. Paul traveled the eastern Mediterranean spreading the Word. In the fourth century CE, the emperor Theodosius made Christianity the official religion of the Roman Empire.

In the eighth and early ninth centuries, Charlemagne (Charles the Great), brought Christianity to pagans and Arians with his military conquests. He spread Christianity from the kingdom of the Franks in Western Europe to an area that ultimately contained what is now France, Switzerland, Belgium, the Netherlands, and parts of Germany, Austria, and Spain. He was crowned Emperor of the Romans by Pope Leo III in 800 CE. As leader of the Holy Roman Empire, Charlemagne encouraged missionary work and the copying of theological manuscripts.

In 1395, John Wycliffe produced the Lollard Bible, marking "the beginning of what may be called the defiantly English translation of the sacred scriptures."[191] Wycliffe's English translation challenged the teachings of the Pope so strongly, one could say that this Bible was the genesis of the Reformation. The cultural history of England also became tied to the Bible. Peter Ackroyd, a prolific writer and Fellow of the Royal Society of Literature, wrote that the "English became, in one favorite phrase, 'the people of the book'."[192]

Johannes Gutenberg, a German goldsmith from Mainz, invented the printing press in 1455, thus enabling the dissemination of information to large segments of the population. His first publication was the two-volume Gutenberg Bible; he produced 200 of them in 1455. The Bible was of such importance that it was the

---

[189] Ibid., 92–6.
[190] Agus, *Jewish Thought*, 82.
[191] Peter Ackroyd, *Albion: The Origins of the English Imagination*, 292.
[192] Ibid.

first book ever to be mass-produced. By 1500, thousands of towns throughout Europe had printing presses. Initial printings of books tended to be religious texts, and so the written word of Christianity moved throughout the continent.

In the sixteenth century, Protestant William Tyndale translated most of the original Hebrew and Greek texts of the Hebrew Bible and Greek New Testament into more modern English, to give the English people a Bible in their own language, rather than in the Latin of the pre-Reformation church. Henry VIII, the monarch who broke with Rome, ordered copies of this English Bible to be placed in every church in England, thus bringing the Protestant Word of God to the masses. The King James Version, 1611, followed in the footsteps of Tyndale. Using this Bible, the Anglican Church spread the Word throughout the British Empire, and its lyrical language, metaphor, and poetry entered the consciousness of millions of people. The Puritans brought the King James Bible to the New World when they landed in Plymouth in 1620.

There is no doubt that many leaders have abused religion for their own purposes, yet the foundation documents of all democracies are connected to the Bible. The Magna Carta of 1215, the touchstone of English liberty, described by Lord Denning as "the greatest constitutional document of all times—the foundation of the freedom of the individual against the arbitrary authority of the despot,"[193] is a continuation of the rights of human beings as promulgated in the Bible and the reminder that no human being has the right to take on the mantle of supreme authority. The former Chief Rabbi of Great Britain, Lord Jonathan Sacks, refers to the teachings of the "three crowns"—priesthood, kingship, and Torah[194]—as "the first statement in history of the principle, set out in the eighteenth century by Montesquieu in *L'Esprit des Lois*, and later made fundamental to the American constitution, of 'the separation of powers' consistent with the fundamental Judaic idea

---

193 Sir Robert Worcester, "Why Commemorate the 800th Anniversary?," MagnaCarta800, http:// magnacarta800th.com/ magna-carta-today/ objectives-of-the-magna-carta-800th-committee/.
194 Lord Jonathan Sacks, "Learning and Leadership," Aish.com, http:// www.aish.com/ tp/ i/ sacks/ 272467251.html.

that leadership is service, not dominion or power or status or superiority."[195]

The leading thinkers of the Renaissance and the Enlightenment continued the progress of science and reason and, although questioning the concept of a personal God, continued to express the importance of freedom and free will and that humankind, as revealed in the Bible, is not under the control of nature, rather we are innovators, or in Biblical parlance, co-creators with God.

The American Declaration of Independence in 1776 incorporated the eighteenth-century ideas of John Locke and Gottfried Wilhelm Leibniz about the God-given freedom of the individual: "We hold these truths to be self-evident, that all men are created equal, that they are endowed by their Creator with certain unalienable Rights, that among these are Life, Liberty and the Pursuit of Happiness."

John Adams, a member of the Declaration of Independence committee and second president of the United States (1797–1801), understood the deep connection between ethical monotheism and freedom.

> *I will insist that the Hebrews have done more to civilize men than any other nation. If I were an atheist, and believed in blind eternal fate, I should still believe that fate had ordained the Jews to be the most essential instrument for civilizing the nations. If I were an atheist of the other sect, who believe or pretend to believe that all is ordered by chance, I should believe that chance had ordered the Jews to preserve and propagate to all mankind the doctrine of a supreme, intelligent, wise, almighty, sovereign of the universe, which I believe to be a great essential principle of all morality, and consequently of all civilization.[196]*

In Europe, the French were promoting the ideas of the Enlightenment in their motto: Liberty, Equality, and Fraternity. Canada, established in 1867, promoted peace, order, and good government and can trace its constitution back to the Magna Carta.

---

195 Ibid.
196 John Adams, Letter to F.A. Van der Kemp, December 27, 1816.

In 1982, when the Canadian constitution was repatriated from Britain, the Canadian Charter of Rights and Freedoms included the statement that "Canada is founded on principles that recognize the Supremacy of God and the rule of law."

President Obama recently said that "while freedom is a gift from God, it must be secured by His people here on Earth." We secure it through our social contract.

We have talked about the effects of our stories and our myths and metaphors on our beliefs and behaviors. For thousands of years, the Bible has been Western civilization's foundational story. It is true that the Bible is not the first book of morals. The Code of Hammurabi came first. But Hammurabi's laws did not show leniency or equality in mercy to those who broke laws: children were killed for the sins of their fathers. So people don't talk about Hammurabi. We talk about God and His commandments: laws that do not distinguish between commoner and noblemen. All citizens are held equally accountable. Individual responsibility is prioritized.

"Whether or not God exists, our genes guarantee that we will bear faith and that our bodies will be soothed by believing in some antithesis to mortality and human frailty."[197] Camus (1913–1960) wrote, "I would rather live my life as if there is a God, and die to find out there is not, than live my life as if there is not and die to find out there is."[198]

For those who wish to remove God from His teachings, would they remove the names of the Founding Fathers of their countries? In the United States of America, the Founding Fathers—George Washington, Benjamin Franklin, Thomas Jefferson—loom large in the psyche of the people. They are wrapped in legend and mythologized. They are entwined with the Declaration of Independence and the Constitution, the documents that comprise the creation story of America.

What would happen if the names on these documents were removed? When the Supreme Court makes rulings, it refers to the

---

[197] Benson, *Timeless Healing*, 198.
[198] Albert Camus, as quoted on Art Quotes, http:// www.art-quotes.com/ getquotes.php?catid=174#.VJr43_8A8.

Constitution and to the Founders in order to provide an historical perspective that adds legitimacy to their decision-making. If the Founders are removed, there is a good possibility that over time the laws will lose their legitimacy, because when a ruling is given, one could respond, "Who says?" Moses Mendelssohn (1729–1786), a noted German philosopher and the grandfather of composer Felix Mendelssohn, wrote that historical truths and events are only witnessed once. We learn of them through those who pass down the information. "Hence the respectability and the trustworthiness of the narrator constitute the sole evidence of historical matters. Without testimony, we cannot be convinced of any historical truth. Without authority, the truth of history vanishes with the occurrence itself."[199]

There is an old story. When God told Moses to announce himself to the Israelites as their God-appointed leader, Moses asked what he should say. Why should the Israelites listen to him? Who was he to tell them what to do? And God told Moses to tell them that "Yahweh, the God of your ancestors, the God of Abraham, the God of Isaac, the God of Jacob, has sent me to you. This is my name for all time, and thus I am to be invoked for all generations to come" (Exodus 3:15). God is entwined in the documents that reveal that all are created equal because we are made in the image of God. Just as one invokes the names of the Founding Fathers of the Constitution to maintain American legitimacy, so too do we invoke God's name with the Judeo-Christian ethic to maintain its legitimacy.

At no point in the Bible are we told that we have no control over our lives. Although God may have a plan for us and may know the outcome in advance, we humans do not.[200] So we must continue to make ethical choices and resist blaming others. Unlike Chuang-Tzu, the Taoist who *flowed* with the river, our metaphor in Western culture is to man the raft and *lead it* down the river, *choosing* the spots to stop, to hunt and gather, to discover, and to co-create.

Some sociologists, such as Peter L. Berger and Thomas Luckmann, believe that we are "denatured, unfinished, world-

[199] Sharon Keller, editor, *The Jews: A Treasury of Art and Literature*, 161.
[200] Weisel, *Messengers*, 79.

open" self-creating creatures, a product of our culture, constructed by the society in which we live.[201] And neuroscience is pointing to many aspects of our personality that appear to be prewired. But somewhere in the middle, we have (at least) a semblance of free will. We can choose to choose. We are not at the mercy of "God's will," where we throw our hands up in the air and say that all is decided for us. That is an excuse for stasis or worse. If, as a culture, we left everything up to God, we would never recover from floods or drought, volcanoes or earthquakes. We would never have had the courage to fly, to go to the moon and beyond searching the universe, and perhaps finding God.

Western culture and ethical monotheism have transformed the world. And the world's greatest transformation has been the knowledge that we humans are individually accountable for our actions. Our failure to succeed is not a result of the demands made by this ethical monotheistic God; it is a result of our failure to live up to those demands.

---

[201] Carveth, *Sociology and Psychoanalysis*, 2.

XXVI
REVELATION

Religion is not myth or magic. It is the recognition of how small we are in the scheme of things, and how great is our responsibility to others.

—Rabbi Jonathan Sacks[202]

I once had the opportunity to attend several lectures by a variety of religious teachers on the subject of healing. One of the speakers questioned God's purpose in revealing the Ten Commandments. Of all the knowledge that He could have imparted to us, the speaker asked, why did God provide such self-evident rules? Why didn't God reveal something more mysterious, perhaps more important, such as the workings of the human brain?

We would have learned that the brain is a miracle of matter, an awesome creation; three pounds of jelly-like material, filled with billions of nerves and trillions of connections that are responsible for how we think, feel, behave, our five senses, movement, and breathing. We would have learned that the deepest part of our brain contains the amygdala, which we hold in common with amphibians and which controls our physical response to fear, and that the middle part of our brain holds our emotions and memory. But we also would have learned that God created us astoundingly different from all His other creations: He gave us a brain that allows us to reason, problem solve, judge, control our impulses, and be the seat of empathy and altruism. Of all of God's creatures, we are the only ones with free will.

If God had told us about the anatomy and functions of the brain instead of giving us the Ten Commandments, would we be better

202 Jonathan Sacks, *Challenging the Idols of the Secular Age*, RabbiSacks.org, http://www.rabbisacks.org/ challenging-the-idols-of-the-secular-age-credo/.

for it today? The commandments against murder, incest, and adultery speak for themselves—but apparently not loudly enough. Coveting destroys relationships and drains the soul. Wanting what others have can lead to murder, adultery, gossip, and dishonoring and abusing our parents. Always seeking and desiring what others have prevents us from enjoying, nurturing, and growing our own garden.

Many pundits today say that common sense dictates that these behaviors are counterproductive to a society, as if common sense were the sixth of our senses and as biologically innate. But if common sense were so common, why do we still fail at keeping the commandments?

Would the world be different today if people had known 3500 years ago that the frontal lobe of the brain, which oversees judgement and impulse control, is not completely developed until the late teens or early twenties? Would the revelation of the internal workings of the brain have prevented murder or bullying while promoting charity and lovingkindness? It seems we are doing much better at unmasking the secrets of the brain, while we still struggle with implementing the seemingly self-evident commandments.

Maybe it is time to take another look at those Ten Commandments and rethink teaching them, in order to counteract our increased sense of entitlement and our selfish, mean-spirited behaviors. Perhaps we can start with the ninth commandment, "You shall not bear false witness": short and simple. Yet truth-stretching, lying, and gossip have become our favorite pastimes: online, on television, and in the schoolyard. Remember the nursery rhyme, "Sticks and stones can break my bones, but names will never hurt me!"? It isn't true. Language is a powerful weapon. Gossiping, name-calling, and lying are destructive, especially today, when an evil word spreads in the blink of an eye through social networking, even violating the sanctity of our homes. It is easier to recover from a broken bone than a broken soul. Schoolchildren do not commit suicide over broken bones.

The purpose of the revelations at Mount Sinai was to impress upon us the importance of compassion if we want to live peacefully within a community. But compassion is not just feelings.

Compassion without action is like whispers in the wind. The commandments help us become more ethical and more spiritual people. They provide the path, the way to develop compassionate behavior, which evolves into empathy when internalized. Perhaps we shouldn't disparage these Ten Commandments until we are no longer in need of them.

A skeptic might ask why a commandment would stop someone from killing. Well, human nature obviously doesn't stop them.

XXVII
GO FORTH

A hard lot has been created for human beings,
a heavy yoke lies on the children of Adam
from the day they come out of their mother's
womb,
till the day they return to the mother of them
all.
What fills them with foreboding and their
hearts with fear
Is dread of the day of death?

Ecclesiasticus 40:1

What is it within us that causes us to fight so tenaciously to live? In death, there is no remembering God. In the grave, one can no longer praise Him. So we battle on. King David did not want to die. His life was too full. The story is told that he thought he could postpone his death by studying, as it was believed that the Angel of Death could not take your life while fulfilling God's commandments. But David's time had come. The Angel of Death needed to distract him just long enough to take his soul. He did. And King David died.

In Judaism, there is a ritual that can be performed in an attempt to fool the Angel of Death. The angel sets out with the names of those whose time has come. By changing your name, it is hoped that you can confuse the angel. In the hope that you will live a long life, the new name that is chosen is usually the name of someone who lived a long life, such as the matriarch Sarah. The decree of death is thus delayed, giving you time to heal.

I remember a young patient asking me to perform this ceremony. We talked for a while and she seemed to feel that she would get better if her name were changed. I have no idea if this young woman truly believed that she could fool the Angel of Death by changing her name. It didn't matter. A new name brings new possibilities. By taking on a new name, you are hoping to take on the attributes of the person whose name you have chosen. You imagine yourself as this person. It is, in a sense, a rebirth, full of opportunity to redefine yourself, even in ill health. After all, God told King Hezekiah, "I have heard your prayer, I have seen your tears. I shall add fifteen years to your life" (Isaiah 38:5). But ultimately, dust shall return to dust.

> *Where now are the leaders of the nations*
> *and those who ruled even the beasts of the earth,*
> *those who sported with the birds of heaven,*
> *those who accumulated silver and gold*
> *on which all people rely*
> *and whose possessions had no end,*
> *those who worked so carefully in silver —*
> *but of whose works no trace can be found?*
> *They have vanished, gone down to Sheol.*

Baruch 2:16–19

Yahweh said to Abram (Abraham), "Leave your country, your kindred and your father's house for a country which I shall show you" (Genesis 12:1–2). So Abram did as he was told. He took his wife, Sarai (Sarah), his nephew Lot, and all the possessions they had amassed (Genesis 12:5–6). The Bible gives us only the bare bones of the story. But within those few lines, we are introduced to a narrative that has stayed with us for millennia, because it was—and remains—life- and world-changing. In those few lines, history changed.

Abram was seventy-five years old when he packed up and left his home for an unknown destination. He took all his possessions. But what could they have been that he was able to take all of them? When we think of the possessions that we can acquire today in seventy-five years, it's almost unimaginable the amount of cartons and the size of the truck we would need to move everything. And Abram made this move to an unknown place based solely on the word of and his faith in this ineffable God.

There comes a time for all of us when God calls to us to "go forth," and we must leave the home we have known all our lives and, like Abraham, go into the unknown. Unlike Abraham, we cannot take our possessions with us. And, ultimately, what we leave behind is far more important than anything we could take with us. What we leave behind will be our legacy: how we want to be remembered at the holiday table when our family gets together to reminisce. We are all told the importance of getting our things in order before we die. We write a will distributing our possessions to our loved ones, trying to think about who would most appreciate this object over that. Now, many of us plan our own funerals and prepay them. But how many of us think about the values, morals, and ethics that we must pass on to our children and grandchildren if they are to carry on and benefit from the traditions of Western culture? How much time have you expended thinking about and writing an ethical will? Your name and your deeds are the greatest possessions which you can leave to your family, as you take your last breath in this world and the first breath in the world to come.

> As a drop of water in the sea, as a grain of sand on the shore are man's few days in eternity. The good things in life last for limited days, but a good name endures forever.
>
> —Ben Sira

> I am standing upon the seashore. A ship at my side spreads her white sails to the morning breeze and starts for the blue ocean. She is an object of beauty and strength. I stand and watch her until at length she hangs like a speck of white cloud just where the sea and sky come to mingle with each other.
>
> Then someone at my side says: "There, she is gone!"
>
> "Gone where?"
>
> Gone from my sight. That is all. She is just as large in mast and hull and spar as she was when she left my side and she is just as able to bear her load of living freight to her destined port. Her diminished size is in me, not in her. And just at that moment when someone at my side said: "There, she is

gone!" there are other eyes watching her coming, and other voices ready to take up the glad shout: "Here she comes!"

—Anonymous

The Father cries, the Son dies, and the Holy Spirit hovers nearby.

And always, we remember them. At the rising of the sun and its going down. At the blowing of the wind and the chill of winter. At the opening of the buds and in the rebirth of the spring. At the blueness of the skies and in the warmth of summer. At the rustling of the leaves and in the beauty of the autumn. The beginning of the year and when it ends. As long as we live, they, too, will live: for they are now part of us, as we remember them.

When we are lost and sick at heart. When we have joy we crave to share. When we have decisions that are difficult to make. When we have achievements that are based on theirs. As long as we live, they will live; for they are now part of us, as we remember them.

—Sylvan Kamens & Rabbi Jack Riemer

XXVIII
REDEMPTION

Yahweh, I called on your name from the deep pit. You heard my voice, do not close your ear to my prayer, to my cry. You are near when I call to you. You said, "Do not be afraid!" Lord, you defended my cause, you have redeemed my life.

Lamentations 3:56–58

I was born in the winter of 1951, in the middle of a flu epidemic. My father couldn't come to visit us, so my mom held me up at the window and my dad—standing in the freezing cold, wearing his coat and hat (a fedora, of course)—looked up at us wistfully.

I came home to an older brother: two and a half years older. I guess my life was pretty regular. I can't seem to remember anything specific about my early years; it's as if while growing up I was there but not there. I went to school. I played in the schoolyard, and knew I had to come home when my mother put the porch light on. We lived next to the school. In those days, children were free to explore and play, without parents hovering nearby. We went skating, visited the zoo, and spent time with family. I remember Halloween. I would go trick-or-treating with my brother.

I was a precocious child. And I remember one day so vividly it's as if it happened yesterday. I was eight or nine. My brother and I were sitting at the kitchen table. We were at opposite ends of the table, occupying ourselves, while Mom stood over the kitchen sink, to the right of me, looking out over the backyard. She was robotically washing the dishes: soapy water, clean water, dish rack. She was there, but not there. I was looking at photo albums. I loved looking at photo albums. This time I noticed that there were two pictures of my brother when he was about two and a half. I could read the dates and was good at math. The problem was that the dates under the photographs were different. "Mom, how come

~ 183 ~

there are two pictures of my brother with different birth dates?" One was my brother, she said, the other was Martin. My other brother. He had died before I was born. He had been the oldest.

Martin. A new name for me. We hadn't talked about Martin. There were no pictures of him in the house. No one in the extended family talked about Martin. So Martin remained a mystery for a long time. At some point before I had my own children, I had learned that Martin had died at two and a half at home, with my mother, my grandmother, the police, the fire department, the ambulance, and the family doctor all in attendance. My dad had been on his way home from downtown Toronto. Martin died from a virulent case of croup. His throat closed and there was nothing they could do. It was so sudden and terrifying that the story was written up in the newspaper, the *Telegram*, which was a major paper in Toronto at the time. My parents stayed in that house and later brought me home to it. Every day of their lives they walked by the place where their first-born son had died.

There is a Hasidic saying, "There is nothing so whole as a broken heart." Is it because the peculiar sadness of compassion is brought forth by broken things, or is the promise of wholeness simply folded into love for the broken?

When I was young, my mother and I would lie down outside on the grass, side by side, and look up at the clouds. She would point here and there and ask, "Do you see an elephant, or a cow, or a butterfly or a whale or anything?" I have fond memories of those times. Looking back, I wonder if the game we played allowed my mother to look for Martin. I also have many memories of my mother standing at the kitchen sink, just like the day she told us about Martin. It's another indelible picture in my head of my mother present, but not really; in quiet contemplation, somewhere else.

There are those who remember my mother as quiet, reserved, cool. Perhaps *distant* is the word they are looking for. I have heard wonderful stories about my mother before she had children. She told these stories, my dad told them, and our friends and family talked about her growing up. She was happy. She was educated and well-traveled, and that was unusual in those days. She had a real zest for life. I saw glimpses of that. She would take us skating and then leave us at the side of the rink and speed off, arms pumping, and then round the corners, one hand behind her back like an Olympic skater.

But I also remember the times when I would get so sick that the doctor had to make a house call. It was always tense when the doctor was called. The next day my aunt from Galt (now Cambridge) would magically appear at my door with soup. She would sit with me until I finished eating. Then my grandmother would look in. My mother and father would be at the periphery. I didn't make all the connections, then. My aunt had two children whom she had left at home so she could come help us; not to help me, really, but my mother. And my grandmother was there for my mother, too. How my grandmother also must have suffered when her daughter's son had died. Once, my mother made a mistake when giving me some pills. I heard my dad get upset and then he left the house, slamming the door behind him. He was afraid of losing another child; afraid of bonding.

I loved my parents and I know they loved me, but growing up I always felt like I lived behind a wall of plastic wrap—there was always something between me and those I loved. A separation. An inability to know or love as deeply as I wanted to know or love. A fear of bonding.

I don't recall talking about Martin at all with my father, Abraham: not until my father was dying. Even then, my dad was in a coma when I mentioned Martin. Each night I would say to my dad before I left the hospital that it was okay for him to die. Not to worry, I would take care of Mom. Everything would be all right; he could go and be with Martin. And then I would say, "But wait until tomorrow." Dad died without me there.

After Dad died, I talked to Mom about Martin. My mother never called Martin by name. She referred to him as "my boy." I would visit his grave and come back and tell her, and she would look up and say, "You saw my boy?" I carried her wistfulness in me; her sorrow, her loss, her emptiness. In an attempt to help my mother, I told her a parable about a little boy who had suddenly died. Everyone wanted a reason for his death. It didn't make sense. A little boy? What had such a little boy done to die so young? Isn't that the universal question?

We are born with a soul. And that soul grows inside a body that is the container for the soul. Sometimes the body gives out before the soul has finished developing. So God, in His infinite wisdom, puts the soul into another body until the soul has completed its growth. Then, when the body is no longer needed to cradle the soul, it returns to God. That's why the little boy died. The soul only needed a place to grow for a short time. I think back on that story. It was a story based on religious beliefs. I get great comfort from those stories. I prefer them to stories I have heard from social workers or psychologists. I don't know what my mother thought. I do know, though, that she died comforted by her religion.

Once, in her later years, my mother told me she believed it was her fault that Martin had died. She said that she had been sleeping at the end of his bed when he was ill, and she had fallen asleep and he had died. I don`t know why she took on that pain and guilt. Perhaps she conflated it with the years of sleeping at the feet of our beds when my brother and I were ill. So I got a copy of the newspaper article about Martin, to show her that she had done everything humanly possible to save him.

Martin died on February 27th. My parents' wedding anniversary was February 28th. I was born February 21st. I think about that and wonder, how could my parents celebrate their anniversary on such a date? But they did. We even surprised them with a party on their 25th anniversary.

I was with my mother when she died. She became ill on a Thursday and was sent to the hospital, but she was able to return to her apartment. By Monday she looked fragile, gray in color, and she was confused. I called the ambulance and I went with her to the hospital. She was kept overnight and then we were told that she was truly unwell, that her lungs were tired. I sat beside her. I watched her as she talked. She was wearing an oxygen mask so I couldn't hear her, but she wasn't talking to me. She was having her own private discussion. I had rested my head on the side of the bed, drifting off into a light sleep like the one that parents develop when that first child comes home, listening to her breathe. I don't know how it happened, but all of a sudden, I was wide awake. Her breathing had changed. It was slower, calm, less congested. Her face had lost all its wrinkles. Her skin was smooth and soft. And then my mother took her last, quiet breath. And her soul slipped away.

I had been told by nurses taking care of my father that some people will not die when their loved ones are there. Others wait for you to come to them before they let go. I don't think there is any scientific data on this. It doesn't matter, really. These are stories we tell to the living to help them with the death of those they love, so they can integrate that death and bear it.

I still visit Martin's grave. I keep him up to date on the family. He's listened to me as I became a parent and then a grandparent. I talk to him as if I have known him forever. And in a strange way, I have. I carry Martin within me. I miss a brother I never met, but seem to know intimately. When he died, so too did the dreams my parents had for him. And then I was born and their dreams for him lived on in me and mingled with mine. And we became one. I internalized Martin. I sometimes think I have lived and am living two lives. I keep him alive.

When a parent loses a child, the sibling who remains loses not only the sibling, but also the parents. I never knew my parents as Martin had. In a sense, I lost my parents, the parents they would have been, before I was born. Before I leave the cemetery, I tell Martin to take care of our parents. And I know in my heart that they are all together, on the right side of God, protected by the wings of the *Shekhina*, the Holy Spirit.

When I last visited my parents' grave, I told them that I don't know how they ever recovered from Martin's death. I continue to be in awe of them. And at that very moment, I pictured in my head a store near me called Recovering Nicely. You take in your tattered couches and chairs and they reupholster them, re-cover them as good as new or even better. By re-covering them, they hide the past by removing it from sight.

People can't be re-covered, and we certainly don't recover nicely after such sorrow. We are not made or created that way. Our past is part of us. If we try to hide it or cover it up, we suffer more. Repressing the past comes back to haunt us in the future. We don't recover. We change, we adjust, we adapt and continue to live. Perhaps it is true that the greatest secret God gave to us was not how to begin, but how to begin, again.[203]

---

[203] Idea taken from Elie Wiesel, *Messengers*, 32.

EPILOGUE
DEUTERONOMY:
THESE ARE THE WORDS

Christianity will go. It will vanish and shrink. I needn't argue about that; I'm right and I will be proved right. [The Beatles are] more popular than Jesus now; I don't know which will go first—rock'n'roll or Christianity. Jesus was all right but his disciples were thick and ordinary. It's them twisting it that ruins it for me.

—John Lennon[204]

It is time to put behind us the childish interpretation of the religion of Adam and Eve of the Garden. As Paul declared: "When I was a child, I used to talk like a child, and see things as a child does, and think like a child; but now I have become an adult, I have finished with all childish ways" (1 Corinthians 13:11). The Bible is far more than its surface meaning, far more than merely a collection of fascinating stories beloved by children. It is a rich, multilayered, multifaceted, deeply profound work of art.

The stories in the Bible provide the path to personal liberation and a nourished soul as well as the infrastructure upon which to build an ethical, compassionate, free, and hopeful society. These stories are classics because they speak to every generation. They speak to all our emotions, all our behaviors, all our yearnings, and to our human existential angst. They lead us to question our choices, our humanity, our values, our accomplishments, and our failures. The Bible teaches us about family relations, community living, and interactions with strangers. Its stories are stories about love and hate, sorrow and joy, murder and deceit, honor, guilt and

---

[204] Ferguson, *Civilization*, 256.

shame, forgiveness, atonement and redemption. Just as the Bible is the story of the human journey—the search for what it means to be human—it is also the story of God's quest for righteousness in humankind.

> *The Bible is a rich, multilayered, multifaceted, deeply profound work of art.*

The Bible entreats us to be our brother's keeper, to behave like Abraham who questioned God and protested on behalf of others, so that we develop, practice, and internalize compassion and empathy. These values are essential for democracy to function, because a just society must at times implement policies that disregard individual wants and needs. The Bible gives us step-by-step instructions on how to establish a society that gives equal weight to individual rights and group responsibilities. And the Bible urges us to not give in to our fears. Fear leads us away from paths of righteousness and into the arms of false messiahs who promise us answers to all our questions. The Bible teaches us not to fear living, relating, revealing, creating. Do not fear, and the past will not hold you back. Do not fear, and the present will give you hope. Do not fear, and the promise of the future will be bright.

Is there reason in these beliefs? More important to me, is there reason to believe? For me, yes. Belief in God provides a way to explain the yearning and the searching for something that we all intrinsically know we once had but that now eludes us. Belief in God provides for hope and possibility even in the presence of evil. Reason insists that creation is the result of evolution: nothing but cold, hard facts. Belief in a compassionate and merciful God expands our awareness of the awesomeness of the universe and everything in it; this belief reminds us of our obligations to each other and to all creatures, great and small. As Elie Wiesel declares, "Faith in God is linked to faith in man, and one cannot be separated from the other."[205]

---

[205] Wiesel, *Messengers*, 91.

Belief in the teachings of the God of Abraham, Isaac, Jacob, and Jesus demands that we welcome the stranger, but it does not demand of us that we welcome all his beliefs and behaviors. It is in the public square that we practice and protect our freedoms and our openness. It is in the privacy of our own homes that we practice our rituals and patterns of worship. Freedom flourishes with hard work and requires constant nurturing.

French intellectual Jean-François Revel cautioned us about the danger of complacency in his book *How Democracies Perish*: "Democracy tends to ignore, even deny, threats to its existence because it loathes doing what is needed to counter them. It awakens only when the danger becomes deadly, imminent, evident. By then, either there is too little time to save itself, or the price of survival has become crushingly high."[206]

We are the caregivers of the teachings of the one God and, as when tending a garden, we must be ever vigilant so that we can distinguish between the behaviors that we want to flourish and those that could overwhelm and destroy the garden.

Life offers us multiple opportunities, multiple ways of seeing, perceiving, understanding, and explaining our outer and inner lives. Life is meant to be lived deeply and loved deeply. It is our opportunity to continue the chain from past to future. We each have the honor of adding something to the world: charity, lovingkindness, empathy. This journey is not meant to be taken alone; we all require assistance. We can turn to psychology and sociology. We can deconstruct language or study philosophy. I suggest religion: the ties that bind us together, one to the other. Not the religion of dogma, but the true essence of religion: honoring the ethical teachings of God and transforming them into compassionate behavior.

In the evolutionary history of humankind, ethical monotheism has been with us for a mere blink in time. Our ancestors arrived around 6 to 8 million years ago. Between two and five million years ago, they began walking on two feet. *Homo erectus* walked in Africa 1.6 million years ago. *Homo sapiens* evolved approximately 300,000

206 Revel, *Democracies*, 4.

years ago and our most direct *Homo sapiens* ancestors approximately 50,000 years ago. The oldest cave art discovered thus far, found in El Castillo, Spain, is 40,800 years ago. Speech developed about 40,000 years ago. The morals and values given to us at Mount Sinai entered our consciousness a mere 3500 years ago; these teachings are in their infancy.

The ancient stories, the ancient lessons of human frailty and moral growth recorded in the Bible and the Gospels, come from a particular time and a particular voice, but these stories—their morals, their values, and their ethics—have been speaking to all of us through the ages. In the Bible, God is reaching out to each one of us personally, beseeching us to listen and to act. But it is up to each one of us to choose: to decide that we will heed His call—or pretend to be deaf.

The lessons of the Bible, the foundation of our culture, will not lose their significance as long as we allow them to teach our minds and touch our souls.

> *The purpose of life is not to be happy. It is to be useful, to be honorable, to be compassionate, to have it make some difference that you have lived and lived well.*

> —Ralph Waldo Emerson

Halleluyah.
Praise God in His holy place,
Praise Him in the heavenly vault of His power,
Praise Him for His mighty deeds,
Praise Him for all His greatness.
Praise Him with fanfare of trumpet,
Praise Him with harp and lyre,
Praise Him with tambourines and dancing,
Praise Him with strings and pipes,
Praise Him with the clamour of cymbals,
Praise Him with triumphant cymbals,
Let everything that breathes praise Yahweh.
Halleluyah.

Psalm 150

BIBLIOGRAPHY

Ackroyd, Peter. *Albion: The Origins of the English Imagination*. London: Chatto & Windus, 2002.

Agus, Jacob B. *The Evolution of Jewish Thought from Biblical Times to the Opening of the Modern Era*. London: Abelar-Schuman, 1959.

Armstrong, Karen, *A History of God: The 4000-Year Quest of Judaism, Christianity and Islam*. New York: Ballantine Books, 1993.

Armstrong, Karen, *The Bible: A Biography*. Vancouver: Douglas and McIntyre Ltd, 2007.

Armstrong, Karen, *The Great Transformation: The World in the time of Buddha, Socrates, Confucius and Jeremiah*. London: Atlantic Books, 2006.

Baron, David. *Sacred Moments*. Beverly Hills, CA: Temple Shalom for the Arts, 2001.

Benson, Herbert, MD. *Timeless Healing*. New York: Scribner, 1996.

Bloom, Allan. The Closing of the American Mind: The Books and School of the Ages. New York: Simon and Schuster, 1987.

Bloom, Harold. *The Western Canon*. New York: Harcourt Brace, 1994.

Boas, Franz. *The Limitations of the Comparative Method of Anthropology*. 1896.

Browne, Janet. *Darwin's Origin of Species: A Biography*. New York: Atlantic Monthly Press, 2006.

Buber, Martin. *On Judaism*. Edited by Nahum N. Glatzer. New York: Schocken Books, 1967.

Cahill, Thomas. *The Gifts of the Jews*. [Garden City, NJ?]: Anchor Books, 1998.

Carveth, Donald. "The Analyst's Metaphors: A Deconstructionist Perspective." *Psychoanalysis & Contemporary Thought* 7, 4 (1984): 491-560.

Carveth, Donald. "Sociology and Psychoanalyis: The Hobbesian Problem Revisited." *Canadian Journal of Sociology* 7, 2 (1982):201-229.

Cohn-Sherbok, Lavinia. *A History of Jewish Civilization*. Secaucus, NJ: Chartwell Books, 1997.

Cohen, M.J. *Pathways Through the Bible*. Philadelphia: Jewish Publication Society of America, 1964.

Cuddihy, John Murray. *The Ordeal of Civility: Freud, Marx, Levi-Strauss, and the Jewish Struggle with Modernity*. Boston: Beacon Press, 1987.

Dimont, Max. *Jews, God, and History*. New York: Penguin, 2004.

Durant, Will. *The Story of Philosophy*. Garden City, NY: Simon and Schuster, 1927.

Earhart, H. Byron, editor. *Religious Traditions of the World*. San Francisco: Harper, 1993.

Faust, Drew Gilpin. *This Republic of Suffering: Death and the American Civil War*. New York: Alfred A. Knopf, 2008.

Fatah, Tarek. *The Jew Is Not My Enemy: Unveiling the Myths That Fuel Muslim Anti-Semitism*. Toronto: McClelland & Stewart, 2010.

Ferguson, Niall. *Civilization: The West and the Rest*. New York: Penguin Group, 2011.

Fletcher, Joseph. *The Ethics of Genetic Control: Ending Reproductive Roulette*. Buffalo: Prometheus Books, 1988.

Fromm, Erich. *You Shall Be As Gods*. New York: Henry Holt and Co., 1966.

Frost Jr., S.E. *Basic Teachings of the Great Philosophers*. New York: Doubleday, 1962.

Gilbert, Martin: *Churchill and the Jews*. New York: Henry Holt and Co, 2007.

Gordis, Daniel. *God Was Not In the Fire*. New York: Scribner, 1995.

Gray, John. *Straw Dogs*. London: Granta Publications, 2002.

Handler, Hetherington, Kelman. *Give Me Your Hand: Traditional and Practical Guidance on Visiting the Sick*. Berkeley: Congregation Netivot Shalom, 1997.

Hertz, Joseph H. *Sayings of the Fathers*. New York: Behrman House, 1945.

Hertzbrg, Arthur, editor. *Judaism: The Unity of the Jewish Spirit Through the Ages*. New York: George Braziller, 1962.

Heschel, Abraham Joshua. *The Insecurity of Freedom: Essays on Human Existence*. New York: Farrar, Straus and Giroux, 1967.

Heschel, Abraham Joshua. *Moral Grandeur and Spiritual Audacity: Essays*. Edited by Susannah Heschel. New York: Farrar, Straus and Giroux, 1996.

Hirsi Ali, Ayaan. *Nomad: From Islam to America: A Personal Journey Through the Clash of Civilizations*. Toronto: Alfred A. Knopf, 2010.

Hoff, Benjamin. *The Tao of Pooh*. New York: Penguin Books, 1982.

Kandel, Eric. "Speaking Memory." *Scientific American Mind*, October 2008.

Keller, Sharon R., editor. *The Jews: A Treasury of Art and Literature*. New York: Hugh Lauter Levin, 1992.

King, Ross. *Machiavelli: Philosopher of Power*. New York: Harper Collins, 2007.

Kushner, Lawrence. *God Was in This Place & I, i Did Not Know*. Woodstock, VT: Jewish Lights Publishing, 1991.

Kushner, Lawrence. *Honey from the Rock*. Woodstock, VT: Jewish Lights Publishing, 1995.

MacIntyre, Alasdair. *After Virtue: A Study in Moral Theory*. Notre Dame, IN: University of Notre Dame Press, 1981.

New Jerusalem Bible, The. New York: Doubleday, 1985.

Noll, Richard. *The Aryan Christ: The Secret Life of Carl Jung*. New York: Random House, 1997.

Pagels, Elaine. *Adam, Eve, and the Serpent*. New York: Random House,1988.
Pagels, Elaine. *Revelations*. New York: Viking, 2012.
Philosophical Library, The. *The Wisdom of Freud*. New York: 1950.

Revel, Jean Francois. *How Democracies Perish*. New York: Harper Perennial, 1985.
Rosner, Fred. *Modern Medicine and Jewish Ethics*. New York: Yeshiva University Press, 1991.

Stanford Encyclopaedia of Philosophy. "Russel, Bertrand." December 1995, revised March 2010.
Sandel, Michael J. *Justice: What's the Right Thing to Do?*. New York: Farrar, Straus, Giroux, 2009.
Scherman, Nosson. *Chumash: The Stone Edition*. Brooklyn: Mesora Publications, 1996.
Sharlet, Jeff. *The Family*. Brisbane, Australia: University of Queensland Press, 2008.
Smith, Huston. *The Religions of Man*. New York: Harper One, 1991.
Soloveitchik, Joseph. *The Lonely Man of Faith*. Jerusalem: Koren Publishers, 2011.
Somerville, Margaret. *The Ethical Imagination: Journeys of the Human Spirit*. Toronto: House of Anansi, 2006.
Spong, John Shelby. *Reclaiming the Bible for a Non-Religious World*. New York: Harper One, 2011.
Steiner, George. *In Bluebeard's Castle*. New Haven, CT: Yale University Press, 1971.
Steiner, George. *Nostalgia for the Absolute*. Montreal: CBC Enterprises/Les Entreprises Radio Canada, 1983.
Stevenson, Leslie. *Seven Theories of Human Nature*. New York and Oxford: Oxford University Press, 1987.
Strathern, Paul. *The Artist, The Philosopher, and The Warrior: The Intersecting Lives of Da Vinci, Machiavelli, and Borgia and the World They Shaped*. London: Vintage, 2009.

Taylor, Jill Bolte. *My Stroke of Insight*. New York: Penguin, 2009.

Visotzky, Burton L. *The Genesis of Ethics*. New York: Three Rivers Press, 1996.

Wiesel, Elie. *Messengers of God*. New York: Touchstone, 1976.
Wistrich, Robert S. *From Ambivalence to Betrayal: The Left, the Jews, and Israel (Studies in Antisemitism)*. Lincoln and London: University of Nebraska Press, 2012.

Made in the USA
Lexington, KY
29 January 2016